Norse Mythology

THE ELDER EDDA
IN PROSE TRANSLATION

Edited by
LAWRENCE S. THOMPSON

Archon Books
1974

Edda Saemundar. English.
　　Norse mythology; the Elder Edda in prose translation.

　　Translation first appeared in the translators' Corpus
poeticum boreale, 1883.
　　I. Gudbrandur Vigfusson, 1827—1889, tr. II. Powell,
Frederick York, 1850—1904, tr. III. Thompson, Lawrence
Sidney, 1916—　　ed. IV. Title.
PT7234.E5G8　1974　　　839'.6'1　　　　　　72-22324
ISBN 0-208-01394-6

© 1974 by Lawrence S. Thompson
First published 1974 as an Archon Book,
an imprint of
The Shoe String Press, Inc.
Hamden, Connecticut

To Sarah

A better philologist than her father

Printed in the United States of America

CONTENTS

INTRODUCTION

The core of Germanic mythology has been preserved in the Elder or Poetic Edda, the name of a corpus of mythical, heroic, and gnomic poems. It is to be distinguished from the Younger or Prose Edda of Snorri Sturluson (1179-1241). The first part of the latter work is a handbook of mythology for the use of poets, in part repetitious of the Poetic Edda. Both the Prose Edda and other sources such as skaldic poetry, the older sagas, and the Gesta Danorum (ca. 1200) of Saxo Grammaticus must be used to elucidate and expand the content of the Poetic Edda. Many of the old poems suffer from serious lacunae and corrupt texts. The purpose of the present compilation is to present the traditions in the Poetic Edda as the point of departure for the study of Germanic mythology. In order to improve the intelligibility of the collection, there are explanatory introductions, and there has been a slight re-arrangement of the traditional sequence of the poems, essentially the policies of mediaeval scribes, but for reasons dictated by a century of modern scholarship. A few poems not in the traditional canon of the Poetic Edda have been included, but they are Eddic in tone and quality and might well have been included but for accidental circumstances of oral and manuscript transmittal.

The age of the individual poems of the Poetic Edda has been the subject of a voluminous scholarly literature. Suffice it to say, there are some aspects of the content which undoubtedly go back to Indo-European antiquity and that there are many striking resemblances to traditions of other Germanic peoples outside of Scandinavia. Certainly many of these traditions were held in common at one time. The actual composition of the Eddic poems is a matter of conjecture, and the dates of 800-1100 A.D. will be given here without any commitment to defend them. Originally the poems were transmitted orally until they were finally written down in the thirteenth century.

There are numerous translations, many in verse which skillfully imitates the originals. However, since the purpose of the present text is to provide access to the content rather than to the style and literary history of the Poetic Edda, the prose translation in the Corpus Poeticum Boreale (1883) of Gudbrand Vigfusson and F. York Powell will be used. A minor disadvantage of using this text is that it translates proper names into forms into which they would normally have developed in English, but this situation will be no great handicap to the perceptive student.

Further reading in secondary materials is strongly recommended. Older works such as Jacob Grimm's Teutonic Mythology, the extensive commentary in Vigfusson and Powell, and P.A. Munch's Norse Mythology are still useful. All are currently available as reprints. Histories of Icelandic literature such as Stefan Einarsson's History of Icelandic Literature (1957) and E.O.G. Turville-Petre's Origins of Icelandic Literature (1953) are recommended. Brian Branston's Gods of the North (1955) is the best recent treatise. Above all, the first part of Snorri's Prose Edda ("Gylfaginning," the beguiling of Gylfi), available in several translations, will help the reader with many difficult or confusing parts of the Poetic Edda. Those who can read German or Scandinavian languages have at their disposal a very extensive literature on ancient Germanic myth, religion, legend, song, and recorded history. Further, a sound knowledge of Latin is necessary in order to use effectively the mediaeval sources such as Saxo.

HÁVAMÁL (WORDS OF THE HIGH ONE)

Most sophisticated religions have sacred or mythical literature containing proverbial wisdom and commentary on social relationships. The ancient Scandinavians had some half dozen poems pulled together under the title of Hávamál, and there are related poems in the Poetic Edda and elsewhere. The Hávamál is believed to have been the sayings of the High One, Odin (Woden, Wotan), mainly because of several strophes which refer to his deeds.

Odin acquired his wisdom by studying runes, the alphabet adopted from the Roman by the Germanic peoples and widely used in Northern Europe during the period before the introduction of Christianity and, indeed, sporadically long thereafter. Those versed in runic lore were often masters of conjure, and women as well as men practiced these arts. Odin also acquired great wisdom from hanging on a gallows tree for nine nights, wounded with a spear. While the specifics of this tradition were surely influenced by missionaries' reports of events in Judaea, the notion of sacrifice by hanging was quite widespread in Germanic antiquity.

In many places there are references to or partial versions of traditions given in more detail elsewhere. Thus one must consult Snorri for the full story of the mead of Suttung (Suptung). Some references, for example, Odin's passion for the daughter of Billing, do not appear elsewhere. Some names and allusions will become clearer after reading further in the Poetic Edda.

The teachings of the Hávamál reappear frequently in the mediaeval literature of Iceland. The thoughts and deeds of the principal figure of one of the great sagas, Egil Skalla-Grímsson, almost amount to a dramatization of the Hávamál. While the poems of the Hávamál probably originated in Norway, they delineate a way of life that that permeated mediaeval Scandinavian civilization from Green—land to Constantinople.

3

1-3. HAIL, mine host! a guest is come, where shall he sit? Hot haste is his that has to try his luck standing at the gate-post. The new-comer with his cold knees needs a fire. A man that has travelled over the hills needs meat and clothing. He that comes to a meal needs water, a towel, a welcome, good fellowship, and a hearing and kind answer if he could get it.

4. A man that travels far needs his wits about him; anything will pass at home. He that knows nought makes himself a gazing-stock when he sits among wise folk.

5. A man that has travelled far, and seen many lands, will know the ways of every kind of men, if he have his wits about him.

6-9. The wary guest who comes to his meal keeps a watchful silence; he listens with his ears, and peers about with his eyes; thus does every wise man look about him.

The fool gapes when in company, mutters to himself, sitting stock still. But if he get a drink, then immediately his mind is all displayed.

A guest that mocks his fellow guest is pleased when he drives the other away. But he that gabbles over a meal, little knows but that his baying will bring his foes upon him. Many men, good friends otherwise, will quarrel over a meal; it will ever be a besetting sin for guest to wrangle with guest.

10-12. Let the cup go round, yet drink thy share of mead; speak fair or not at all. No one can blame thee for ill-breeding though thou go early to sleep.

A glutton, unless he has his senses about him, eats himself into life-long misery. The fool's belly makes him a laughing-stock in company of gentle-folk.

The flocks know their time of folding, and leave their pasture: but a fool never knows the measure of his own belly.

13-14. Blessed is he who wins a good report and the favour of men: for it is hard to win over other men's hearts.

Blessed is he who in his life enjoys good report and good advice: for many a man has suffered from another's evil counsel.

15-16. No man can bear better baggage on his way than wisdom; in strange places it is better than wealth. It is the wretched man's comfort.

No one can bear a better baggage on his way than wisdom; no worse wallet can he carry on his way than ale-bibbing.

17. He feels at his ease who can ask and answer. The sons of men can keep silence of nothing that passes among men.

18. He that never is silent talks much folly. A glib tongue, unless it be bridled, will often talk a man into trouble.

19. It is a far way to an ill friend, even though he live on one's road; but to a good friend there is a short cut, even though he live far off.

20. One's own home is the best, though it be but a cottage. A man is a man in his own house. Though thou hast but two goats and a hut of hurdles, yet that is better than begging.

21. One's home is the best, though it be but a cottage. A man is a man in his own house. His heart bleeds who must beg for every meal.

4

22. I never met with a man so open-handed and free with his food but that boon was boon to him; nor so [prodigal] as not to look for return if he had a chance.

23. To one man's house I came much too early, to another's much too late; either the ale was drunk out, or it was unbrewed. An unwelcome guest always misses the feast.

24. Here and there I should have been bidden had I known where to look for my next meal; or if even two hams were hanging at my good friend's for every one I had eaten.

25. Once I was young, and travelled alone, then I went astray. I felt happy when I met a man. Man is man's comfort.

26. Open-handed bold-hearted men live most happily, they never feel care; but a fool troubles himself about everything. The niggard pines for gifts.

27. I bestowed my raiment on two men of wood in the field; they looked gallant when they were dressed. A naked man is bashful.

28. The young fir in a court withers; neither bark nor shoots shelter her. Even so is a man whom nobody loves. Why should he live long?

29. The eagle coming to the sea sniffs and droops her head over the ocean. Even so is the man who comes into company having no comrades.

30. Hotter than fire for five days flares friendship between ill friends; but when the sixth day comes it is slaked, and all friendliness turns sour.

31. Brand kindles brand till it is burnt out; fire is lit from fire. Through speech man draws nearer to man, but becomes wilful in proud loneliness.

32. He that opens all his heart to another mixes blood with him. . . .

33. Only one's own mind knows what lies in one's heart; a man is his own confidant. No sorrow is worse to a man than to be able to enjoy nothing.

34. Fire is the goodliest thing the sons of men can have, and the sight of the sun, the enjoyment of good health, and a guileless life.

35. A man is not utterly wretched though he have ill health; some men are blessed with sons, some with kindred, some with wealth, some with good deeds.

36. Better be quick than dead. A live man may always get a cow. . . .

37. The halt may ride a horse; the handless may drive a herd; the deaf may fight and do well; better be blind than buried. A corpse is good for nought.

38. A son, though late born after his father's death, is better than none. Few road-stones stand by the wayside that were not raised by son for father.

39. Chattels die; kinsmen pass away; one dies oneself: but good report never dies from the man that gained it.

40. Chattels die; kinsmen die; one dies oneself: I know one thing that never dies, a dead man's name [good or bad].

41. No man is so good but there is a flaw in him, nor so bad as to be good for nothing.

5

42. Little are grains of sand; little are drops of water; little are men's minds: for all men were not made wise alike. The average of men is but moiety.

43. He that knows nought else knows this, many are befooled by riches. One is wealthy, another needy, never blame a man for that. . . .

44. I saw fire consume the rich man's dwelling, and himself lying dead before his door. . . .

45. Anything is better than to be false. He is no friend who only speaks to please.

46. Dry logs and bark-flakes, wood to last for all meals and seasons, one knows how to husband them. But . . . [the application is missing].

47. . . . One often has to pay dear for [idle] words spoken to another.

48–55. The fool thinks he shall live for ever if he keeps out of battle: but old age gives him no quarter, though the spears may.

A fool is awake all night worrying about everything; when the morning comes he is worn out, and all his troubles just as before.

A fool thinks all that smile on him his friends, not knowing, when he is with wise men, what there may be plotting against him.

A fool thinks all that smile on him his friends; but when he goes into court he shall find few advocates.

A fool thinks he knows everything, if he sits snug in his little corner. But he is at loss for words if people put him on his mettle.

A fool, when he comes among men, 'tis best he hold his peace. No one can tell that he knows nothing unless he talks too much; for a fool is a fool still speak he ever so much.

A fool if he wins wealth or woman's love waxes in pride, but not in wisdom, and goes on steadily in his own conceit.

The miserable man whose mind is warped laughs at everything; knowing not what he ought to know, that he has no lack of faults.

II.

56. A king's son should be silent and thoughtful, and daring in battle; cheery and blithe every one should be till his death-day come.

57. Every man of foresight should use his power with moderation; for he will find when he comes among valiant men that no man is peerless.

58. Middling wise should every man be, never over-wise. Those who know many things fairly lead the happiest life.

59. Middling wise should every man be, never over-wise. No man should know his fate beforehand; so shall he live freest from care.

60. Middling wise should a man be, never too wise. For a wise man's heart is seldom glad, if its owner be a true sage.

61. A man should be merry at home and cheerful with his guests, genial, of good manners and ready speech, if he will be held a man of parts. A good man is in every one's mouth. Archdunce is he who can speak nought, for that is the mark of a fool.

62–66. No man should blame another in matters of love; hues charmingly fair may move the wise and not the dullard. Never blame a man for what is all men's weakness. Mighty love turns the sons of men from wise to fools.

6

The man who will win a lady's grace should speak fair and offer gifts and praise the fair maid's form. He that woos will win.

No man should trust a maiden's talk, nor any woman's word; for their hearts were wrought upon a whirling wheel, and falsehood planted in their bosoms.

Now I will make a clean breast of it, for I know quite well that men's mind to women is false; we speak fairest when we mean falsest; this beguiles honest souls.

67–71. A man should be a friend to his friend, and pay back gift with gift; give back laughter for laughter, and leasing for lies.

A man should be a friend to his friend, to himself and his friend; but no man should be a friend of his foe's friend.

Friends should gladden one another with gifts of weapons and raiments, such as may shew about one's body. 'Give' and 'give back' make the longest friends, if there be luck withal. Give not overmuch at a time; one often buys a friend at little outlay; I got a comrade with half a loaf and the last drops of my cup. . . Gift always looks for return.

72. The wise man, who wishes to be called well bred, must both ask and speak:—(The latter part is here wrong. Better, 'A wise man should learn to answer all questions.')

Tell one man [thy secret] but not two; what three know all the world knows.

73. He should rise betimes who has few workers and get about his work; many hindrances has he who sleeps his mornings away; wakeful man's wealth is half won.

74. He should rise betimes that would win another's chattel or life. The slumbering wolf seldom gets a joint; nor the sleeping man victory.

75. Go on, be not a guest ever in the same house. Welcome becomes Wearisome if he sit too long at another's table.

76. A man should not step a foot beyond his weapons, for he can never tell where, on his path without, he may need his spear.

77. A man, ere he goes in, should look to and espy all doorways; for he can never know where foes may be sitting in another man's house.

78. A man should take his meal betimes, before he goes to his neighbour, or he will sit and snuffle, like one starving, and have no power to talk.

79. Washed and fed should a man ride to court, though he be not so well clad; let none be ashamed of his shoes or breeches, nor of his horse though it be but a sorry one.

80. A man should not boast of his wits, but rather keep watch over his mind, when a wise and silent man comes to a house. The wary man will seldom slip; for there is no better friend than great common sense.

81. A man should not make a gazing-stock of another in company; many a man feels happy when no one asks him questions, and he may keep his corner with a dry skin.

82. A man should not stint himself of money he has made; the loathed often get what was meant for the loved. Things often go worse than was hoped.

This is a fragment found only in one manuscript, but, since it logically belongs with the Hávamál and may, indeed, once have been a part of it, it is inserted here.

1–3. PRAISE the day at eventide; a woman at her burying; a blade when it is tried; a maid when she is married; ice when crossed; ale when drunk.

4–5. Fell wood in a wind; row out in fair weather; court a maid in the dark. Many are the day's eyes.

6–7. A ship for speed; a shield for shelter; a sword for a stroke; a maid for marriage.

8–10. Drink ale by the fireside; slide on the ice; buy a lean horse and a rusty blade; fatten thy horse at home and thy hound at thine house.

11–24. A creaking bow; a burning low; a gaping wolf; a coughing crow; a grunting sow; a rootless tree; a waxing wave; a boiling cauldron; a flying shaft; a falling billow; ice one night old; a coiled snake; a bride's bed-talk; a broken sword; a bear's play, or a king's child; a sick calf; a self-willed thrall; a sibyl's fair oracle; a fresh-felled corpse, or thy brother's killer though thou meetest him abroad; a half-burned house, or a swift steed; a steed is useless if but one leg is broken. Let no man be so confident as to trust in any of these things.

25-28. Let no man trust an early-sown acre, nor too soon in a son: weather makes the acre, and wit the son; each of them is slippery enough.

29–33. The love of a woman whose heart is false, is like driving with a slip-shod, wild, two-year old, badly broken horse on slippery ice; or sailing in a rudderless ship with a gale behind her; or like setting a lame man to catch a reindeer on the thawing hill-sides.

34–39. Wherever thou drinkest ale take earth's strength [as antidote]: for earth acts against ale; and fire against sicknesses; oak against binding of the bowels; the corn-ear against witchcraft; spur of rye against hernia;—call on the moon against curses;—heather against biting sicknesses; runes against charms. Earth drinks up floods.

40–44. He who trusts in his wallet is glad when the night sets in. Short are ship's berths. An autumn night is changeable. The weather often changes in five days, but oftener in a month.

45–46. Two are never on one side. The tongue works death to the head. A stout hand is often hid under a shabby cloak.

47–50. From the tread of the cat, from a woman's beard, from fishes' breath, and birds' milk, from a hill's roots, and a bear's tail: out of all these things Gleipni (the Lithe Shackle) was fashioned.

Like the Song of Saws, the counsels given to the youthful Loddfáfnir appear only in one manuscript. The usual didactic elements concerning personal conduct are so closely related to the Song of Saws that they are inserted here.

1. I COUNSEL thee, Loddfafni; do thou take my counsels; they will profit thee if thou take them; and do thee good if thou followest them: Rise not at night, save thou be scouting, or go out to cover thy feet.

2. I counsel thee, etc.: Sleep thou not in a witch's arms lest she palsy thy limbs. She will make thee to forget the assembly and the king's business. Thou shalt refuse thy meat, and all pastime of men, and go off sorrowful to sleep.

3. I counsel thee...: Never tempt another man's wife to be thy mistress.

4. I counsel thee . . .: If thou art minded to travel on fell or firth, take good provender with thee.

5. I counsel thee . . .: Never let a bad man know thy mishaps: for of a bad man thou shalt never get good reward for thy sincerity.

6. I counsel thee . . .: Know this, if thou hast a trusty friend, go and see him often; because a road which is seldom trod gets choked with brambles and high grass.

7. I counsel thee . . .: Draw a good man to thee for thy good conversation, and learn spells of good favour whilst thou livest.

8. I counsel thee...: Be not thou the first to break off with thy friend. Sorrow will eat thy heart if thou lackest a friend to open thy heart to.

9. I counsel thee...: If thou hast a friend in whom thou trustest, and thou wishest to profit by him, mingle souls with him, and exchange gifts with him, and go and see him oft. If thou hast another in whom thou trustest not, and yet thou wilt profit by him, thou shalt speak fair to him and mean false, and pay him leasing with lies. Farther, smile thou in the face of him thou trustest not, and whose faith thou suspectest, and speak against thy mind. So shall gift pay back gift.

10. I counsel thee . . .: Never bandy words with mindless apes, for thou wilt never get good reward from an ill man's mouth; but a good man will make thee strong in good favour and man's goodwill.

11. I counsel thee . . .: Do not speak three angry words with a worse man; for often the better man falls by the worse man's sword.

12. I counsel thee . . .: Be thou neither shoe-smith nor shaft-smith save for thyself: if the shoe be misshapen or the shaft be wry, thou shalt get ill thanks.

13. I counsel thee . . .: Where thou encounterest a curse invoke the moon against it, and give no peace to thy enemies.

14. I counsel thee . . .: Never rejoice at evil; and be of good conversation.

15. I counsel thee . . .: Never look up in battle: the sons of men may be turned into swine [panic-stricken]; beware of men spell-binding thee.

16. I counsel thee . . . : If thou wilt converse with a good woman, and take thy pleasure with her, thou shalt promise fair and hold to it. No one will turn away from good.

17. I counsel thee . . . : I bid thee be wary, and yet not over wary; be wary with ale and with another's wife; and thirdly, lest thieves play a trick with thee.

18. I counsel thee . . . : Mock thou not nor laugh at a guest or a way-farer, for often no one in the house knows who they may be that come.

19. I counsel thee . . . : Never laugh at a hoary sage: old men's sayings are often good; discreet words often come out of a shrivelled skin, hanging among the hides, and dangling among the pelts, and swinging among the bondsmen.

20. I counsel thee . . . : Never growl at a guest, nor drive him from thy gate. Be kind to the poor. There is might in the door beam, which shall swing for all men's coming. Set a ring (a handle) thereon, or it shall bring down curses on thine every limb.

21. O Loddfafnir! long shalt thou need these songs; may they be good to thee if thou follow them, profitable if thou receive them, gainful if thou trust them!

ODIN'S LOVE LESSONS

This fragment of the story of the beguiling of Suttung and his daughter in order to obtain the mead that gives poetic inspiration is found in full detail in Snorri. It is included with the Hávamál poems for lack of a better place for it in the Eddic corpus as we have it.

1. MANY a good maid, if thou knowest her well, turns out false to a man. I proved that when I tried to lead the wise maiden astray, the gentle lady mocked me throughout, I got no favour from her.

2–7. I proved that when I sat in the rushes, watching for my love; I thought there was no happiness for a man but in her sweet body; the gentle maid was as my own flesh and blood, yet she was not mine. I found the sun-white Billing's daughter sleeping in her bed. 'Come then, Wodin, in the gloaming, if thou wouldest talk with me. It would be my ruin if any but us two knew of our unlawful love.' Away I went, I was distraught with love; I was sure I should win her whole heart and love. But when I came again, all the armed household was awake with burning lights and flaming torches; such a woeful walk had I. And nigh morning-tide, when I came again, and all the household were asleep, then I found the fair lady's hound tied to her bed.

8–10. I sought the old Giant,—now I am back. It was not by hold-ing my tongue that I won my suit there; many a word I spoke to my profit in Suptung's hall. Gundfled gave me to drink of the pre-cious mead in a golden chair; I gave her back evil reward for her true heart, and for her steadfast love. I let the point of Rati (the auger) make its way gnawing through the rock. Giant causeways were over and under me. Thus I risked my head.

11–12. The fraud-bought mead has profited me well. The wise man lacks nought now that Odreari [Inspiration] is come up to the skirts of the city of men. I doubt whether I should have come back out of Giant-town had I not had the help of Gundfled, that fair lady in whose arms I lay.

13. Next day the Frost-giant came . . . asking for Balework, if he were back among the gods, whether Suptung had sacrificed him.

14. Wodin, I ween, had taken the oath on the ring; how shall his good faith be trusted any more! He betrayed Suptung out of his mead, and made Gundfled weep.

15. The heron of forgetfulness hovers over banquets; he steals away the minds of men. I was fettered with that bird's feathers in Gundfled's mansion.

16–17. I was drunk, I was over-drunk at the wise Fialar's [the Dwarf]. The only comfort is that a man's wits (wandering through drink) come home again. The ale of the sons of men is not so good as it is said to be, for the more a man drinks the less he is master of his wits.

THE OLD RITUAL

This mystical and liturgical fragment is the final part of the Hávamál group of poems assembled by Vigfusson and Powell. Fragmentary as it is, it does give some notion of what may be a ritual of considerable antiquity, possibly shared by all the early Germanic peoples.

1. IT is time to speak from the Wiseman's chair. At Weird's Brook, I saw and was silent; I saw and took thought; I listened to men's counsels. I heard them consider the mysteries; nor did they leave words of forethought unspoken in the High One's Hall. In the Hall of the High One thus I heard spoken :—

Woden (the High One) speaks:

2–5. I mind me hanging on the gallows-tree nine whole nights, wounded with the spear, offered to Woden, myself to myself; on the tree, whose roots no man knoweth. They gave me no loaf; they held no horn to me. I peered down, I caught the mysteries up with a cry, then I fell back [descended]. I learnt nine songs of might from Balethorn's son, Bestla's father, and I got the draught of the precious mead, blent with Odreari [Inspiration]. Then I became fruitful and wise, and waxed great and flourished; word followed fast on word with me, and work followed fast on work with me.

6. Thou shalt discover mysteries and staves to read, most great staves, most steadfast staves, which the mighty Wiseman painted and the High Gods made and the Counsel of the Powers graved; Woden among Anses, Dain among Elves, Dwale among Dwarves, Alwise among Giants. I myself graved some.

7. Knowest thou how to grave? knowest thou how to read? knowest thou how to paint? knowest thou how to inquire? knowest thou how to play? knowest thou how to sacrifice? knowest thou how to send? knowest thou how to offer?

8. Better is never graved than graved out of measure, etc. . . . .

Thus Thund [the Great Sage] graved ere the world began.

Now I ascended returning again.

9. I know songs, such as no King's daughter, nor son of man knows. *Help* the first is called, it will help thee with all suits and sorrows, and all kinds of sickness.

10. A second one I know, which the children of men need who wish for healing simples. . . .

11. A third one I know: If I am in sore need of bonds for my enemies, I can deaden my enemies' swords, their swords will bite no more than staves.

12. A fourth I know: If my foemen lay bonds on my limbs, I can chant myself free; the fetter flies off my feet, and the shackles off my hands.

13. A fifth I know: If I see a shaft shot with deadly aim into the ranks; fly it never so fast I can stay it, if my eyes light on it.

14. A sixth I know: If a man wounds me by spells of a . . . tree; the curse shall bite him that lays the spells upon me rather than me.

15. A seventh I know: If I see a hall aflame over the sleepers, be the flame ever so broad I can stay it. Such a charm know I how to chant.

16. An eighth I know (most profitable to men): Whereso feud arises among princes, I can heal it forthwith.

17. A ninth I know: If I am in need to save my ship afloat, I still the wind on the waves, and lull the whole sea.

18. The tenth I know: If I see witches [hedge-riders] dancing in the air, I prevail so that they go astray and cannot find their own skins and their own haunts.

19. The eleventh I know: If I am to lead my old friends to battle, I chant under the shields, so that they go in their might hale to the battle, hale from the battle, hale wherever they go.

20. The twelfth I know: If I see a halter-corpse swinging high on the tree, I can so grave and paint in signs, that the man shall come down and talk with me.

21. The thirteenth I know: If I sprinkle water on a young lord, he shall never fall though he go to battle, he will be proof against the swords.

22. The fourteenth I know: If I am to tell over the tale of the gods before the host, I know them all well, both Anses and Elves: few dunces know so much as that.

23. The fifteenth I know: How Great Sage (Thiodrearer) the dwarf chanted before Delling's doors; he chanted strength into the Anses, and victory to the Elves, wisdom to the God of Counsel.

24. The sixteenth I know: If I would win a goodly lady's whole heart and love; I can change the white-armed lady's heart, and turn all her love to me.

25. The seventeenth I know: That the young maid shall never forsake me. . . .

26. The eighteenth I know, which I never will tell, neither to maid nor matron,—It is safest to keep one's own secret. This is the end of my Lay—save only to her who lies in my arms, or to my sister.

27. Now the Lay of the High One has been chanted in the Hall of the High One, most profitable to children of men, most unprofitable to the sons of the Giants. Hail to him that spoke it! Hail to him that knows it! Joy to him that learnt it! Hail to them that have listened to it!

VOLOSPÁ (THE SIBYL'S PROPHECY)

Even though the text is obscure and corrupt in many places, this poem is a key document of Germanic mythology. It is a Genesis and an eschatology with much that comes between. There are references to some myths that do not appear elsewhere in the Poetic Edda, e.g., the creation story. Other allusions are to gods and mythical personalities whose deeds and character will be elaborated elsewhere.

There are striking similarities to other religions, notably Christianity and Finno-Ugric shamanism. This situation has influenced some scholars to postulate influences from these sources. The scribes (but probably not most of the original authors) of the Eddic poems knew Christianity and could use its terminology, but there is abundant evidence that their basic material antedates any Christian missions in the north. As far as Finnish and Lapp influence is concerned, any peoples who mix ethnically, regardless of the difference in social and cultural levels, influence one another (note the transmission of Uncle Remus' originally African stories to the Southern white folklore, or their intrusion into folklore of the Cherokees, with whom runaway Georgia slaves often took refuge). The Finns and the Lapps, dominated by more sophisticated neighbors, absorbed far more than they gave. It should be observed that Finno-Ugric scholars have found nothing similar to the Volospá beyond the Urals, but that Greek, Irish, and Semitic myths have much that is similar.

It seems likely that the Volospá is to a considerable extent the Germanic version of original Indo-European myth and that the author was a heathen in the days when Christianity was beginning to penetrate the north. His work might have been intended as a vindication and exposition of the old religion. It is not beyond the realm of possibility that, like Snorri, he was a Christian antiquarian. Whatever the true situation, the Volospá is an authentic picture of the religion of the viking age.

It is of interest to note that the Volospá must have been composed in Iceland. In the case of most of the Eddic poems we cannot say for sure whether they were written in Iceland or Norway. However, the the author of the Volospá knew fire-spouting volcanos, wide sandy beaches, and high rock palisades, a landscape remote from the forests of the mainland.

FOR a hearing I pray all Holy Beings [Gods], and the sons of Heimdall high and low [all men]. Thou O Wal-Father [Woden] wouldst have me set forth in order the histories of men as far back as I remember. I remember the Giants born of yore, who bred me up long ago. I remember nine Worlds, nine Sibyls, a glorious Judge beneath the earth.

In the beginning, when naught was, there was neither sand nor sea nor the cold waves, nor was earth to be seen nor heaven above. There was a Yawning Chasm [chaos], but grass nowhere, ere that the sons of Bor, who made the blessed earth, raised the flat ground. Then the Sun shone forth from the south on the dwelling-stones, and the fields were mantled with green herbs. The Sun from the south, with the moon her fellow, cast her right hand on the edge of Heaven [entered the gates of the horizon]. The Sun knew not her inn, nor the Moon his dominion, nor the Stars their place.

Then all the Powers, the most high Gods, assembled to their judgment-seats and took counsel together, giving names to Night and the New Moons [phases of Moons]: they called Morningtide and Midday, Afternoon and Eventide by their names, for the counting of seasons.

The Anses met on Ida-plain, and raised high places and temples, setting forges, and fashioning treasures, shaping tongs and making tools. They played at tables in the court and were happy, they lacked not gold till there came three most loathsome Titan maids from Giant-land.

*   *   *   *   *   *   *

Then all the Powers, the most high Gods, assembled to their judgment-seats and took counsel together, who should create Dwarf-kind from the bloody surf and the Giants' black bones; they fashioned out of earth, in the image of man, many Dwarves as Durinn commanded.

*   *   *   *   *   *   *

Till out of this host there came to the house three Anses, mighty and blessed. They found Ask and Embla helpless and futureless on the ground. The breath of life was not in them, they had neither feeling nor motion, nor utterance, nor comely hues. Woden gave the breath of life, Hœnir feeling, Lodur utterance and comely hues.

I know an Ash, a high-towering Holy Tree, called Ygg-drasil [Woden's steed, gallows], besprinkled with white loam; whence come the dews that fall in the dales. It spreads ever green over the Weird's burn; whence come the Three Virgins of manifold wisdom, from the Well beneath the tree. They have laid down the fate, and chosen the life and spoken the destinies of the children of men.

The first war in the world that I [the Sibyl] remember was when they speared Gold-weig [Gold-draught], and burnt her in the High One's Hall; thrice was she burnt, and thrice reborn, though still she lives.

*   *   *   *   *   *   *

Then all the Powers, the most high Gods, assembled to their judgment-seats and took counsel together, whether the Anses should pay tribute, or were they to exchange hostages and make a league. Woden hurled *spears* and shot into the host. This was the first war in the world. The paled-wall of the Burgh of the Anses was broken, the Wanes [Gods] marched over the plains that rung with war.

Then all the Powers, the most high Gods, assembled to their judgment-seats and took counsel together *to know* who had charged the air with noisome venom and given the Maid of Od [Freya] to Giant-kind. Thor alone was swelling with wrath, he seldom sits still when he hears such news. Then were utterly broken all oaths and plighted faith and mighty leagues sworn between them.

II. Wheresoever she came to a house they called her Haid, the sooth-saying Sibyl; she charmed divining rods, she knew witchcraft, she was aye the delight of the evil Bride [Hell].

The Father of Hosts endowed her with rings and necklaces, with cunning treasure-spells and rods of divination. She could see far and wide through all the worlds. She could see the Wal-choosers travelling afar, ready to ride to God-folk.

She was sitting alone without when the aged Patriarch of the Anses [Woden] came and looked into her eyes. What ask ye me? Why tempt ye me? I know it all, O Woden, where thou hiddest thine eye in the holy Well of Mimi, who quaffs mead every morning from Wal-Father's pledge.—Know ye yet or what?

I [the Sibyl] know the trumpet-blast of Heimdal, hid beneath the wide-shadowing Holy Tree. I see a stream rush in rapids over the pledge of Wal-Father.—Know ye yet or what?

I behold Fate looming for Balder, Woden's son, the bloody victim. There stands the Mistletoe slender and delicate, blooming high above the ground. Out of this shoot, so slender to look on, there shall grow a harmful fateful shaft. Hod shall shoot it, but Frigga in Fen-hall shall weep over the woe of Wal-hall.—Know ye yet or what?

I behold a captive lying under Cauldron-holt, the bodily semblance of Loki the guileful. There Sigyn sits, sad of heart, over her husband.—Know ye yet or what?

Eastward in Ironwood the aged witch is sitting, breeding the brood of Fenri [the Wolf-ogre], from whom there shall spring one amongst them all in ogre shape that shall pitch the Moon *out of Heaven*. He shall feed on the lives of death-doomed mortals, spattering the heavens with red blood. The sunshine shall wax dark, nor shall any summer follow, and all the winds shall turn to blight.—Know ye yet or what?

On a mound there sat striking a harp the giantesses' shepherd, Egg-theow the Gladsome; in Gaggle-brake, a bright-red chanticleer whose name is Fialar was crowing to her. The cock Gold-comb is crowing to the Anses, waking the warriors of the Father of Hosts. Another cock, Sooty-red, crows under the earth in the halls of Hell.—Fiercely Garm [the hell-hound] bays before the cave of the Rock, the chain shall snap and the Wolf range free!

Tales-a-many the Sibyl can tell. I see farther in the future, the mighty Doom of the blessed Gods. Brothers shall fight and slay one another, kinsfolk shall break the bonds of kindred. It shall go hard with the world: much of whoredom, an age of axes, an age of swords, shields shall be cloven, an age of storm, an age of wolves, ere the world falls in ruin. The sons of Mimi are astir, the Judge is moving at the blast of the Horn of Roaring. Loud blows Heimdal, the Horn is on

16

high, Woden talks with Mimi's head, the towering Ash Ygg-drasil quivers, the aged tree groans, the Giants have broken loose.—Fiercely bays Garm, etc.

How do the Anses fare? How do the Elves fare? All Giant-land is rumbling from end to end. The Anses are assembled. The Dwarves are moaning before their doors of stone, the inmates of the rocks.—Know ye yet or what?

The Giant Hrym comes driving from the east; high he holds his linden shield; the Monster Dragon writhes in giant-fury; the Serpent lashes the waves; the Eagle screams; Pale-neb [the vulture] tears the corpses; Nail-board [the Ship of Doom] is launched. A bark is speeding from the west; the sons of Muspell [the World-Destroyers] are crossing the sea, with Loki for steersman. All the Demons are marching with the Wolf; Byleist's brother [Loki] is in their ranks.

From the south comes Giant Swart, fire in hand; the sword of the Demon of Death shines like the sun. The granite-rocks are rending, the ravines fall in, the Dead are marching up the road of Hell, the Heavens are riven.—Fiercely bays Garm, etc.

Hlin's second woe shall now come to pass when Woden goes forth to fight with the Wolf, and Beli's bright slayer [Frey] encounters Swart. Frigga's darling must die there. Then shall Widar, mighty son of the Father of Hosts, go forth to fight the Beast. He shall thrust his sword down the Monster's jaws right to the heart. Then is his father avenged.

Then shall Hlodyn's glorious child, Woden's son [Thor], go forth to fight with the Dragon. Earth's Holy Warder shall slay him in his might. Nine paces back from the accursed serpent reels the Son of Earth [Thor].

The inmates of Hell [the evil dead] shall all sweep over the earth. . . .

The sun turns to darkness, Earth sinks into the deep, the bright stars vanish from out the heavens, fume and flame rage together, the lofty blaze plays against the very heavens.—Fiercely bays Garm, etc.

III. I behold Earth rise again with its evergreen forests out of the deep; the waters fall in rapids; above hovers the eagle, that fisher of the falls. The Anses meet on Ida-plain, they talk of the mighty Earth-serpent, and remember the great decrees, and the ancient mysteries of Fimbul-ty [the unknown God]. There shall be found in the grass wonderful golden tables, their own in days of yore. The fields un-sown shall yield their increase. All sorrows shall be healed. Balder shall come back. Balder and Hod shall dwell in Woden's mansions of Bliss, in the holy places of the blessed Gods.—Know ye yet or what?

Then shall Hœni choose the rods of divination *aright*, and the sons of the Twin-brethren shall inhabit the wide world of the winds.—Know ye yet or what?

I see a hall, brighter than the sun, shingled with gold, standing on Gem-lea. The righteous shall dwell therein and live in bliss for ever.

Northward in the mounts of Darkness [No-Moon] stands a hall of gold, hostel of Dwarves. But on Okoln [Uncold] stands another, called Surf [Brimi], the Giant's drinking-hall.

Far from the sun on Corse-strand I behold a hall, whose doors stand northwards. In through its luffer drops of venom are falling, its roof is thatched with adders. A river, called Slide, *whose waters are* knives and swords, flows through Venom Dales. There shall the murderers and the mansworn wade through heavy streams, while Nidhogg [Backbiter] the serpent is sucking the corses of the dead, and a Wolf is ravening on men.—Know ye yet or what?

Hither comes Nidhogg, the dark Dragon, the fiery serpent winging his way up from the hills of Darkness, flying over the earth with corses on his wings.

Now must the Sibyl sink.

VAFTHRÚDNISMÁL (WORDS OF VAFTHRÚDNIR)

The Vaftrúdnismál is didactic like the Hávamál but also a treatise on myth like the Volospá. Odin, just as Zeus, usually assumed a disguise on his trips in quest of wisdom, and so he did when he visited the gaint Vafthrúdnir. In the course of the dialogue the latter answered Odin's questions and described the universe, even predicting Ragnarǫk (Fall of the Gods, Goetterdaemmerung) and Odin's death. But Odin asked him the ultimate question of which he alone could know the answer, "What did Odin whisper into the ear of his son (Balder) when he was put on the funeral pyre?"

Note the contrast in the cosmogony of the author of this poem and that of the pre-Socratic philosophers of Greece. The Vafthrúdnismál represents folk belief, while the surviving fragments of the early Greek philosophers are the seeds of metaphysical speculation.

FIRST SCENE.—*Lidskialf in Walhall. Woden and Frigg.*

1. *Woden.* Counsel me, Frigg, now I am longing to visit Wafthrudni (Webstrong). I have a great mind to cap staves of old with that wise Giant.—*Frigg.* I counsel thee, Father of hosts, to stay at home in the seat of the gods. For I never knew of a giant so wise as Wafthrudni.— *Woden.* Far have I travelled, much have I seen, many beings have I known; but now I will find out how Wafthrudni's household stands.— *Frigg.* Farewell in thy going! farewell in thy coming back! farewell on thy way! may thy wits stand thee in good stead, when thou, Sire of men, hast to cap words with the Giant.

SECOND SCENE.—*Giantland, in the Giant's hall, Woden standing before Wafthrudni.*

5. *Woden.* I greet thee now, Wafthrudni! I am come here to thy hall to see thee. First, I must know if thou art a wise and learned Giant.—*Wafthr.* Who is this man that speaks to me in my hall? Thou shalt never leave this hall alive except thou prove the wiser of us two. —*Woden.* Ganger is my name; I am just come off the road thirsty to thy hall. I have yearned on my long journey for thy bidding and hospitality, O Giant.—*Wafthr.* Why dost thou stand and speak from the floor? take thy seat in the hall! Now shall it be proved who is the wiser, the Guest or the old Sage.—*Woden.* When a poor man comes to a rich man, let him speak something to the point or else hold his peace. Great babbling turns to ill, when one encounters a cold-hearted man.

10. *Wafthr.* Tell me, Ganger, as thou wilt try thy luck from the floor, What is that horse called, that draws every day over mankind?—

19

Woden. Sheenmane is its name, the horse that draws the bright day over mankind. The Red-Goths hold him the best of horses; ever glimmers that steed's mane.

12. *Wafthr.* Tell me, Ganger, etc., What is that steed called that draws the night from east over the blessed Powers?—*Woden.* Rimemane is the horse called, which, etc. Every morning the foam drops from his mouth; hence comes the dew in the valleys.

14. *Wafthr.* Tell me, G., etc., What is the river called which parts the land between the sons of Giants and the Gods?—*Woden.* Ifing its name is, etc. Open it runs for ever; no ice comes on it.

16. *Wafthr.* Tell me, G., etc., What is that plain called where Swart and the sweet gods shall gather for battle?—*Woden.* Wigrid that plain is called, etc. A hundred miles it is every way. This is their pitched battle-field.

18. *Wafthr.* Thou art wise indeed, O guest. Come up to my bench, and let us sit and talk together! Guest, let us wager our heads on our wisdom.

Now comes the real trial, and Woden's turn to question.

19. *Woden.* Tell me, firstly, O Wafthrudni, if thy wisdom can tell it thee, and thou knowest it, Whence came the Earth or the Heavens above in the beginning, thou wise Giant?—*Wafthr.* Out of Ymis' flesh the earth was made, and the mountains from his bones; the heavens from the skull of that rime-cold giant; but from his blood the sea; and from his brows the blithe gods made the earth for the sons of men; but from his brains were all the threatening clouds made.

21. *Woden.* Secondly, tell me, etc., Whence the Moon is come that rides above men, and the Sun likewise?—*Wafthr.* Mundilfori (Fireauger) was the father of the Moon and also of the Sun; they must wheel round the heavens every day to tell men the seasons.

23. *Woden.* Thirdly, tell, etc., Whence the Day came that passes over mankind, and the Night with her new moons?—*Wafthr.* Delling is the name of the father of Day; but Night was Norwi's daughter. The blessed gods shaped the full moons (ny) and new moons (nid) to tell men the seasons.

25. *Woden.* Fourthly, tell me, etc., Whence came the Winter and the warm Summer in the beginning, among the wise Powers?—*Wafthr.* Wind-chill is the name of the father of Winter, but Sweet-mood of Summer. . . .

27. *Woden.* Fifthly, tell me, etc., Which of the Giants or the sons of Ymi was the eldest in the beginning?—*Wafthr.* Winters unnumbered ere earth was fashioned was Berwhelm born; Thrudwhelm was his father, and Orwhelm his grandsire.

29. *Woden.* Sixthly, tell me, etc., Whence did Orwhelm come among Giant-kind in the beginning, thou wise Giant?—*Wafthr.* From the Bay of Sleet poisonous drops beat, which grew into a giant. Thence is the whole of our race sprung; hence it is altogether grisly.

31. *Woden.* Seventhly, tell me, etc., How did this sturdy giant beget sons, since he knew not giantess?—*Wafthr.* A maid-child and man-child grew together from under his arm-pit. Foot begat with foot a six-headed son to that wise giant.

20

33. *Woden*. Eighthly, tell me, etc., What earliest thou knowest, and what thou rememberest furthest back, thou wise Giant?—*Wafthr*. Winters unnumbered ere Earth was fashioned Berwhelm was born. The first thing I know of is when this wise giant was laid in the Ark.

35. *Woden*. Ninthly, tell me, etc., Whence comes the Wind, which blows over waves, but is never seen?—*Wafthr*. Carrion-gulper is he called, a giant in eagle's shape, that sits at the end of heaven; from under his wings the wind that blows over all men is said to come.

37. *Woden*. Tenthly, tell me, etc., Whence Niord from Noatun came among the Anses; he rules over countless temples and high places; yet he was not Anse-born?—*Wafthr*. In Wane-world the wise Powers made him, and gave him to the Gods (Anses) for a hostage. In the doom of the Age he shall come back again home to the wise Wanes.

39. *Woden*. Tell me, eleventh, etc.... (*mangled text*).—*Wafthr*. All the Chosen Host in Woden's Court meet together in sword-play every day; they choose the slain, and ride from the battle, and then sit down at peace together.

41. *Woden*. Twelfthly, tell me, Why thou, Wafthrudni, knowest all the fate of the Gods? Thou speakest most truly of the mysteries of the Giants and all the Gods, thou all-wise Giant.—*Wafthr*. Of the mysteries of the Giants and all the Gods I can speak truly, for I have been in every world, I have been in nine worlds, (even) underneath the Hell of Clouds. Hither die the men from Hell (a second death).

43. *Woden*. Far have I travelled, tried untold things, explored untold worlds, etc.: What men shall be left alive when the Monster-winter has passed away?—*Wafthr*. Lif [Sample] and Lifthrasi shall be hidden away in Hoardmimi's holt. They shall feed on the dews of morning and from thence a new generation shall spring.

45. *Woden*. Far have I, etc.: Whence shall come the Sun on their burnished heaven, when the Wolf shall have destroyed this one?—*Wafthr*. The Sun shall bear a daughter ere the Wolf destroy her; that maid shall ride, when the powers have passed away, along the paths of her mother.

47. *Woden*. Far have I, etc.: Who are the maids, the wise-minded, who ride above the mariners?—*Wafthr*. Three great rivers fall over the croft of the Maids of Mogthrasi (the Fates). Only their images are in the world, whilst they themselves dwell with the Giants.

49. *Woden*. Far have I, etc.: Which of the Anses shall own the dominion of the Gods, when Swart's Fire is quenched?—*Wafthr*. Widar and Wali shall inhabit the city of the Gods, when Swart's fire is quenched; Mood and Main shall have Miollni [the Hammer] after Wingni's (Thor's) last battle.

51. *Woden*. Far have I, etc.: What shall be the death of Woden, when the powers fall in ruin?—*Wafthr*. The Wolf shall swallow the Sire of Men; Widar shall revenge him, he shall rend the cold jaws of the Beast and slay him.

53. *Woden*. Far have I, etc.: What did Woden whisper in his son's ear before he mounted the Pyre?—*Wafthr*. No being knows what thou long ago didst whisper in thy son's ear. With a doomed mouth have I set forth my old lore, and the world's doom, now that I have striven in speech with Woden. Thou shalt be ever the wisest of all!

21

GRÍMNISMÁL (WORDS OF GRÍMNIR)

Similar to the Vafthrúdnismál, the Words of Grímnir (the hooded or masked one; see the end of the poem for a partial catalog of Odin's names) is another popular cosmogony. It is built into a story which is related in prose in the manuscripts. Briefly, two sons of a king, Agnar and Geirrod, were stranded when fishing and were sheltered over the winter by a farmer and his wife, none other than Odin and Frigg. In the spring Odin gave them a boat to go home; but, upon their arrival home, Geirrod pushed the boat back into the sea with Agnar and cursed him, "May the trolls take you!"

Agnar went to live with a sorceress, but Geirrod succeeded his father as king. He had the reputation of being stingy and cruel, and Odin went to verify this rumor. Odin would give only his assumed name, Grímnir, and Geirrod put him between two fires for eight nights in order to make him talk. On the ninth the king's ten-year-old son, Agnar, named for his uncle, brought Odin a beaker of mead. The suffering Odin-Grímnir blessed the compassionate youngster, imparted to him a treasury of old lore (the burden of our text), promised that he would have his father's kingdom, and finally revealed his identity.

THE SCENE, *Grimni* (*Woden in disguise*) *in the hall of King Geirrod, staked between two fires, without food or drink. Agnar, the King's son, hands the prisoner a goblet of wine. Then Woden breaks forth into song,—*

1. *Grimni.*—HOT thou art, flame, and far too great! Fall back from me, flame! My fur is singed, though I hold it aloft. My fur burns on me. (*Here Agnar reaches him the cup.*)

2. *Woden.* Hail to thee, Agnar, the God of men bids thee hail. Never for one draught shalt thou get better guerdon. (*Here Woden breaks forth in song*):—

3-16. A holy land I see nigh Anses and Elves. Ever in *Thrudham* Thor shall dwell till the fall of the Powers. *Yewdales* they are called where Wuldor has built him a hall; *Elfham* the Gods gave to Frey in olden time for a tooth-fee. There is the third mansion, which the blessed Gods thatched with silver: it is called *Wale-shelf*, the Anse (Thor) bought it in the olden time. *Sunkbench* the fourth is called, where the cold waves ever murmur above; there Woden and the Seeress drink every day joyfully out of golden cups. *Gladham* the fifth is called, where the gold-bright wide *Walhall* towers; there the Sage (Woden) chooses every day weapon-dead men. That hall is very easy to know for all that come to visit Woden; the house is raftered with shafts, the hall is thatched with shields, the benches are strewn with mail-coats. That hall is, etc. A wolf

22

hangs before the west door, an eagle hovers above it. *Thrymham* the sixth is called, where Thiazi dwelt, that foul giant; but Skathi, the fair bride of the Gods, now dwells in her father's old home. *Broad-blink* is the seventh, there Balder has made him a hall; the land in which the fewest curses lie [the most blessed of lands]. *Heavenhold* is the eighth, where they say Heimdall rules over the fane; here the glad watchman of the Gods drinks the goodly mead in the peaceful hall. *Folking* is the ninth, where Freyja orders the seats in the hall: she chooses half the slain every day, but Woden the other half. *Glistener* is the tenth, its pillars are of gold and it is thatched with silver: here Forseti (Judge) lives every day, settling all causes. *Noaton* is the eleventh; there Niord has built him a hall; the guileless helper of men rules a high-timbered altar-place.

Wood, the land of Widar, is overgrown with sprouts and high grass; here the son [shall mount on] horseback to avenge his father.

17. (. . . . . one verse).

18–19. *Wal-gate* is the gate's name: it stands on the holy plain before the holy doors. It is an ancient gate, but few know how it is locked. Five hundred and forty doors there are to Wal-hall I ween. Eight hundred of the Chosen shall go out of each door at one time, when they go forth to fight the Beast.

20–21. *Heathrun* is the name of the goat that stands on the hall of the Father of Hosts and bites at the boughs of Learad (a tree). She shall fill a vat with pure mead which shall never fail. *Oakthorn* is the name of the hart that stands on the hall of the Father of Hosts and bites at the boughs of Learad: his horns drip into the Boiling-cauldron [Tartarus], whence come all the rivers on earth. . . .

22–23. Kormth and Wormth and the two Charlocks Thor must wade every day when he goes to court at the ash *Ygg's-steed*, for the Anse-bridge burns all aflame, and the holy waters bellow. Gleed and Gylli, Gler and Skidbrim, Silvertop and Sini, Hostage and Fallow-hoof, Goldcrest and Lightfoot, these steeds the Anses ride every day when they go to court at the ash *Ygg's-steed*.

24–29. Three roots stretch three ways under the ash Ygg's-steed. Hell dwells under one, the Frost Giants under the second, mortal men under the third. [An eagle sits in the branches of the ash Ygg's-steed, called . . . ., and between his eyes sits a hawk, that is called *Weather-pale*.] *Rat-tusk* is the name of the squirrel that runs up and down the ash Ygg's-steed: he carries the Eagle's words down and tells them to the Serpent below. There are four bow-necked Harts that gnaw the [high shoots]: Dain and Dwalin, Duneyr and Durathror. More serpents lie under the ash Ygg's-steed than any foolish ape can know: Goin and Moin the sons of Grave-wolf, Greyback and Gravedigger, O. and S., I know will for ever be boring at the roots of the tree. The ash Ygg's-steed suffers greater hardships than men know of. The hart bites its root, and its side is rotting, the Serpent crops it below.

30–32. The speedy *Earlywaker* and *Allswift* draw the Sun hence, and under their shoulders the blissful powers, the Anses, hid the cooling of iron. *Cooler* is the name of the shield that stands before that shining Goddess the Sun. Rocks and sea would burn up, I know, if it fell down. *Skulk* is the name of the wolf that follows the fair-faced Goddess to . . . . But the other is called *Hastener;* he is the son of the Great Beast: he has to run before the bright bride of Heaven. . . .

33. He has the favour of Wuldor and all the Gods who first touches the fire; for all worlds stand open before the Anses' sons when the kettles are lifted. . . .

34–36. *The end of the song. Here Woden reveals himself.*

Woden. Drunk art thou, Geirrod, too deep hast thou drunken. 'Tis grievous for thee to have forfeited my fellowship, that of all the Chosen Host, and Woden's friendship. Often I told thee, but little thou mindedst it. Thy friends are betraying thee; I see my friend's [thy] sword all dripping with blood. Now Woden shall soon have thy sword-worn corse, I know that thy life is at an end, the Sisters frown on thee. Now thou seest Woden. Come nigh me if thou canst! (*Geirrod rises from the fire, and stumbles over his sword, which runs him through.*)

APPENDIX.

BREATH-SOOTY cooks Sea-sooty [the hog] in Fire-sooty [the kettle], the best of bacon, but few know what the Host of the Chosen live on.

2–3. The glorious war-wont Father of Hosts feeds *Greedy* and *Fierce* [his two Wolves], but the weapon-blessed Woden lives on wine alone. *Thought* and *Mind* [his two Ravens] fly every day over the mighty earth: I fear for *Thought* lest he never come back, but I am still more fearful about *Mind*. . . .

4–5. Five hundred and forty rooms in all there are in *Clear-twinkling*. I ween of all roofed halls my son's (Thor's) is the biggest.

I will have Hrist and Mist (Walkyries) to give me the horn. S. and S. etc.; these serve ale to the Chosen Host.

6. The sons of Iwald in the days of old set about building Skidblade, the best of ships, for the bright Frey, the blessed son of Niord.

[Some reference to Eager's banquet.]

8–12. I was called Grim [mask]. I was called Traveller, Host-leader, Helm-bearer, etc. I never had one name since I walked among the natives. They called me Hooded at Geirrad's, Ialk at Asmund's, Keeler when I drew the sledges, Thro at assemblies, Widur in battle, ... Wish and Sough, Even-high and Sway-shield, ... Wizard and Hoar-beard among the Gods. Swithur and Swithri I was called at Sunk-Mimis [the giant of the abyss], when I fooled the old giant, when single-handed I became the slayer of that famous son of Midwolf. Now I am called Woden, before that I was called Awe, and before that I was called Sage, Waker, etc. Gaut and Ialk among the Gods, Opener and Sleep-maker, ... which, I think, all meet in me.

24

ALVÍSSMÁL (WORDS OF ALVÍSS, "ALLWISE")

Alvíss apparently tricked the gods into promising him a wife (a daughter of Thor? Freya?), but they were reluctant to meet their obligations. One of the gods, either Odin or Thor, managed to delay Alvíss by playing on his pride in his wisdom. The interrogator asked a continuous stream of questions to permit Alvíss to display his knowledge, keeping him busy until dawn, when the rays of the morning sun destroyed him. Alvíss' answers consisted of a glossary of synonyms for for the thirteen words which were most important in the life of the mediaeval Scandinavians: Earth, sky, moon, sun, clouds, wind, calm, sea, fire, wood, night, corn, and ale. It is of some interest to note that the words used by man for each thing are the common ones of everyday speech; by the gods, archaic or unusual words; and by the giants, exotic or foreign words. Synonyms used by dwarves and elves are highly imaginative, not inappropriate to the subterranean or ethereal worlds assigned to them in the cosmogony.

FIRST SCENE.—*The door of the Dwarf's cavern. He hurries in hot haste to fetch his bride, telling his servants, as he leaves, to make ready for the wedding feast.*

Allwise (to his men): DECK the benches; the bride will soon be back with me. I am in great hurry for marriage, folk will say. There is no staying at home for me!

SECOND SCENE.—*Outside Walhall. Allwise meets Woden (Wing-thor, Wingi?).*

W. What fellow is this? why art thou pale about the nose? wast thou sleeping with corpses? There is something oger-like about thee; thou art but a sorry bridegroom!—*A.* Allwise my name is. I dwell beneath the earth; under the rock is my homestead; I am come to fetch my bride. Let none break his plighted word.—*W.* I will break it; I have the bride in ward like a father. I was not at home when she was betrothed; I who hallow the weddings of the Gods.

A. Who is the fellow who claims to be the ward of the fair beaming maid ....? *W.* A runagate; nobody knew thee. Who hath bribed thee?—*W.* Wing-thor (Wingi) is my name; I have travelled far; I am Longbeard's son. Without my will thou shalt never have that young maid, nor make that match.—*A.* I would rather have thy goodwill, and make that match; I would sooner win than lack the drift-white maid.— *W.* The maiden's love shall not be denied thee, thou wise guest, if thou canst tell me of every world what I want to know.

25

(Here Dialogue begins.)

W. Tell me, Allwise, for thou Dwarf, methinks, knowest the whole history of mankind :—How is EARTH, which lies before sons of men, called in every world?—*A.* 'Earth' among men; 'Field' among Anses; the Wanes call it 'Way,' the Giants 'Ever-green,' the Elves 'Growing;' the High Gods call it 'Clay.'

W. Tell me, Allwise, etc. How is HEAVEN the . . . . called in every world?—*A.* 'Heaven' among Men, 'Warmer' among Gods; the Wanes call it 'Wind-woof,' the Giants 'High-home,' the Elves 'Fair-roof,' the Dwarves 'Drip-hall.'

W. Tell me, Allwise, etc. How is the MOON, that all men see, called in each of the worlds?—*A.* 'Moon' among Men, 'Mylin' among the Gods; 'Whirling-wheel' in Hell; 'Hastener' the Giants, 'Sheen' the Dwarves, 'Year-teller' the Elves call it.

W. Tell me, Allwise, etc. How is the SUN, that all men see, called in each of the worlds?—*A.* 'Sol' among Men, 'Sun' among Gods; the Dwarves call her 'Dwale's doll;' 'Everglow' the Giants, 'Fair-wheel' the Elves, 'All-sheer' the sons of Anses.

W. Tell me, Allwise, etc. How are the CLOUDS, that are mingled with showers, called in each of the worlds?—*A.* 'Sky' among Men, 'Shower-boder' among Gods; the Wanes call it 'Windfloe,' 'Wet-boder' the Giants; Elves 'Weather-main;' in Hell they call it 'Helm-of-Darkness.'

W. Tell me, Allwise, etc. How is the WIND, that travels so far, called in each of the worlds?—*A.* 'Wind' among Men, 'Waverer' among Gods; the Strong Powers call it 'Neigher,' 'Whooper' the Giants, 'Softgale' the Elves; in Hell they call it 'Whistle-gust.'

W. Tell me, Allwise, etc. How is the CALM, that rests, called in each of the worlds?—*A.* 'Loun' it is called among Men, and 'Lea' among Gods; the Wanes call it 'Wind-slack,' 'Sultry' the Giants, the Elves 'Soul-of-Day ;' the Dwarves call it 'Day's-rest.'

W. Tell me then, Allwise, etc. What is the MAIN, which men row over, called in each world?—*A.* 'Sea' among Men, 'Level' among Gods; the Wanes call it 'Wave,' Giants 'Sound-ham,' the Elves 'Sea-blink ;' the Dwarves call it 'Deep.'

W. Tell me, Allwise, etc. How is FIRE, that burns before the sons of men, called in each of the worlds?—*A.* 'Eild' among Men, 'Fire' among Gods; the Wanes call it 'Wavy,' 'Greedy' the Giants, 'Furnace fire' the Dwarves; in Hell they call it 'Destroyer.'

W. Tell it me, Allwise, etc. How the WOOD, that grows before the sons of men, is called in each of the worlds?—*A.* 'Wood' among Men, 'Wield-fur' among the Gods; the Men in Hell call it 'Cliff-wrack ;' Giants call it 'Firewood,' the Elves 'Fair-foliage ;' the Wanes call it 'Wand.'

W. Tell me this, Allwise, etc. How is NIGHT, Norwi's daughter, called in each of the worlds ?—*A.* 'Night' among Men, 'Newl' among Gods; 'Mask' the Great Powers, 'Unlight' the Giants, 'Sleep-joy' the Elves; the Dwarves call it 'Dream-fairy.'

W. Tell me then, Allwise, etc. How is the SEED, which the sons of men sow, called in each of the worlds?—*A.* 'Bigg' among Men,

'Bear' (barley) among Gods; 'Waxth' the Wanes call it, 'Oat' the Giants, the Elves 'Lees-staff;' in Hell they call it 'Blight.'

W. Tell me then, Allwise, etc. How is the ALE, the sons of men drink, called in each of the worlds?—*A*. 'Ale' among Men, 'Beer' among Anses; 'Draught' the Wanes; 'Clear-lees' the Giants, 'Mead' in Hell; Suttungs' sons (Dwarves) call it 'Good-Cheer.'

W. In one man's breast I never saw more olden words.—With great wiles thou hast, I swear, been beguiled. The Day is upon thee, Dwarf; the hall is full of sunshine! (*The Dwarf is turned into stone.*)

SVIPDAGSMÁL (WORDS OF SVIPDAG)

The background for this didactic poem, preserved only in seventeenth-century copies, is deeply rooted in the fairy tale tradition. The wicked stepmother, the princess in the enchanted castle, and the devoted mother who gives her son advice from the other world are familiar. With charms imparted to him by his departed mother, Svipdag rode on to Giant Land to win his betrothed. This romantic theme was developed into the Danish and Swedish ballads of Sveidal or Svendal.

Vigfusson and Powell state that the story is "probably a Sun-Myth from some alien source" (note that Svipdagr means "Swift Day" and Menglod means "Necklace Glad"). Omitted from our translation is a part involving a magic sword (cf. Skírnismál, infra), possibly a phallic symbol. Whatever interpretations are put on the story, the text itself is significant as one more compilation of old Scandinavian wisdom and charm lore. The Svipdagsmál is not in the Eddic corpus of the older manuscript tradition, but its content must be studied along with the other didactic pieces.

FIRST SCENE.—*At his mother's grave.*

S. AWAKE thou, Groa! awake thou, sweet lady! I bid thee awake at the door of the dead. Perchance thou rememberest how thou toldest thy son to come to the grave-mound.

The Mother. What is it that troubles thee, my only son? what ails thee, that thou callest thy mother, who is turned to dust, and gone from the world of men?

S. That false woman, who lies in my father's arms (my step-mother) has set an ill game for me; she bade me go . . . . to find Menglad.

Mother. Long is the journey, long are the paths; long are the sorrows of men; perchance thou may get thy will, and the fates turn well for thee.

S. Chant me chants, that will help; Mother, save thy child, else I shall perish in my journey; I am but a youth.

Mother. The first charm I chant thee, it will stand thee in good stead; Wrind chanted it to Wali: Cast off from thy shoulder whatever evil thou encounterest; let thyself be thy guide.

The second charm I chant thee: If despair fall upon thee on thy way, may Guarding-charms fence thee about on all sides, as thou goest on thy way.

The third I chant thee: If great waters threaten to overwhelm thee, may flood and foam turn back to Hell the while, and dry up before thee.

The fourth I chant thee: If foes stand in ambush on the gallows-

28

path, mayest thou turn the heart of thine enemies, and shape all their mind to goodwill to thee.

The fifth I chant thee: If fetters be laid on thy limbs, then may my loosing spell make them slip off thy body, the bonds snap off thy limbs, and the fetters off thy feet.

The sixth I chant thee: If thou comest on sea swelling higher than men can tell, may calm and still obey thy bidding, and give thee a peaceful journey.

The seventh I chant thee: If frost overtakes thee high on the mountains, may the winter cold not harm thy body, nor any ill take hold of thy limbs.

The eighth I chant thee : If the night overtake thee on a path of darkness, may the [evil] night-riding witches have no power to come and harm thee.

The ninth I chant thee: If thou must needs bandy words with the goad-wielding Giant, may speech and wisdom be abundantly given into thy heart and mind.

Fare thou well through every danger; may no evil stop thy desire. I stood within doors on the earthfast stone, while I chanted thee these charms. Do thou, my child, bear thy mother's words hence, and let them dwell in thy breast; for ever-abounding luck shalt thou have through thy life as long as thou rememberest my words.

SECOND SCENE.—*Swipday in Giantland, before Menglad's flame-bound bower, encounters the Giant Warder Manywise.*

S. What monster is this, standing in front of the fore-court and wandering round the hot flame?

Giant. What dost thou seek, and what art thou in quest of, and what wouldst thou, lone man, know? Tread back the wet ways; thou hast no abiding-place here.

S. What monster is this that stands in the front of the fore-court, giving no welcome to wayfarers . . .?

G. Manywise my name is; I have a wise mind, though I am chary of my meat; thou shalt never come within these walls, but shalt wander forth like a wolf to the woods.

S. One yearns for the delight of one's eyes, seeing a sweet sight. The courts gleam, methinks, in these golden halls. Here would I live for ever.

G. Tell me, whom wast thou born of, lad, and whose man's child art thou?

S. Wind-cold is my name, Spring-cold was my father's name, Hard-cold his father.

(Here begin the questions.)

Tell me now, Muchwise, what I shall ask, and what I would know: Who rules here and reigns over this land and gleesome halls?

G. Menglad is her name, whom her mother bore to the son of S., she rules, etc.

• • • • • • • • • • • •

S. Tell me now, Muchwise, etc. What is the rock called, on which I see the most belauded maid sit?

G. Hill of Healing it is called, it has long been the joy of the sick and sore. Any woman that climbs it, though she have a year's sickness on her, will become whole.

S. Tell me, M. etc. What are the maids called that sit together peacefully at Menglad's knees?

G. The name, (*all healing names.*)

S. Tell me, M. etc. Whether they deliver those that worship them, if need be?

G. Every summer, if they be worshipped in an altar-hallowed place, though never so high peril overtake the sons of men, they will deliver them every one from his need.

S. Tell me this, M. etc. If there be any one, to whom it is granted to sleep in Menglad's sweet arms?

G. To none of men is it granted to sleep in Menglad's sweet arms, save to Swipday alone; the sunbright bride was destined to him for wife.

S. Push open the door, throw back the gates, lo, Swipday is here! yet go and see if Menglad will have my love.

G. (*shouting to within*). Hearken, Menglad! here is a new comer, go and see the guest; the hounds welcome him, the house has sprung open of itself; I think it is Swipday.

Menglad (*from within to the Giant*). May the great ravens tear out thine eyes on the high gallows-tree, if this be a lie that my love is come from afar to my hall. (*Swipday comes in, she turns to him*): Whence didst thou start? whence didst thou journey? what did thy household call thee? I must have sure token of thy kindred and name, to know whether I be thy fated wife.

S. Swipday is my name, Sunbright was my father's name; the winds have driven me far along cold paths. No one can withstand the word of the Fate, even though it be spoken to one's destruction.

Menglad. Be welcome now! I have got my will; take a kiss with my greeting. A blessed sight is the meeting of two lovers. Long have I sat upon the Hill of Healing, day after day I waited for thee. Now that which I yearned for is come to pass, and thou, my love, art come to my bower. I have yearned sorely for thy kiss, and thou for my love. Now it is true that we shall pass our lives and days together.

GÁTUR GESTUMBLINDA (RIDDLES OF GESTUMBLINDI)

Preserved in the Hervarar Saga along with a few other gems of poetry comparable to those in the canon of the Poetic Edda, this is the oldest collection of Scandinavian riddles. As a blind wanderer (Gestumblindi) Odin visited the court of King Heidrek, famous as a reader of riddles, at Yuletide. Heidrek managed to provide a solution to all the riddles except the ultimate one, the same that was the downfall of Vafthrúdnir in his contest with Odin. Like Vafthrúdnir and Alvíss, Heidrek was a victim of his overweaning pride in his wisdom and must therefore forfeit his life. In common with many other collections of riddles in various early folk traditions, this one is miscellaneous and not grouped by subject.

Guest. 1. Would I had what I had yesterday! guess thou what it was: Men's damager, words' hinderer, and yet words' arouser. Read my riddle, O King Heidrek!—*Ale.*

2. I came from home, I wended my way from home, I saw a way of ways; way underneath, way above head, way on all sides. Read my, etc.—*A bridge.*

3. What drink was it I drank yesterday; it was neither wine nor water, nor mead, nor beer, nor aught of meat kind; yet I went thirstless away? Read my, etc.—*The dew.*

4. Who is that shrill one, who walks by hard paths, having passed them many a time; he kisses very fast, has two mouths, walks on nought but gold? Read my, etc.—*The goldsmith's hammer.*

5. Who is the huge one, who passes over the earth, swallowing water and woods; he fears the wind, but no man, and wages war on the sun? Read my, etc.—*The fog.*

6. Who is the big one, who wades in the deep, turning half towards Hell; he saves people, but tugs against the earth, if he has a trusty withy by him? Read my, etc.—*The anchor.*

7. Who dwells in high mountains? Who falls into deep dales? Who lives without breath? Who is never silent? Read my, etc.—*The raven, the dew, a fish, a fall.*

8. What was that wonder I saw outside Delling's door (outside the hall): It turns its head towards Hell, and its feet towards the Sun? Read my, etc.—*The leek.*

9. What was that wonder, etc.: Two ever-stirring yet lifeless things were boiling a wound-leek? Read my, etc.—*Smith's bellows forging a sword.*

10. What was that wonder, etc.: The white flyers beat the rock, while the black ones are embedded in the sand? Read my, etc.—*Hail and rain.*

31

11. What was that wonder, etc.: I saw a black hog wallow in the mud, though no bristles were on his back? Read my, etc.—*A dung-beetle.*

12. What was that wonder, etc.: It has ten tongues, twenty eyes, forty feet; this being moves along? Read my, etc.—*A sow with a litter of nine pigs.*

13. What was that wonder, etc.: It flies high aloft, yelling loud....? Read my, etc.—*An arrow.*

14. What was that wonder, etc.: It has eight feet, four eyes, carrying its knees higher than its belly? Read my, etc.—*A spider.*

15. What was that wonder, etc.: It lightens people over all lands, and yet is ever chased by wolves? Read my, etc.—*The sun.*

16. What was that wonder, etc.: Harder than horn, blacker than a raven, whiter than egg-film, straighter than a shaft? Read my, etc.—*A streaked agate or obsidian.*

17. Blond-haired brides, bondswomen both, carried ale to the barn; the casks were not turned with hands, nor forged by hammers; she that made it strutted about outside the isles? Read my, etc.—*Eider duck's eggs.*

18. Who are those fairies of the mighty mountains; woman begets by a woman; a maid bears a son by a maid. Those goodwives have no husband? Read my, etc.—*Two Angelicas.*

19. Who are the maids that fight weaponless around their lord; the brown ever sheltering, the fair ever attacking him? Read my, etc.—*The pieces of a table* (hnef-tafl).

20. Who are the merry maids that glide above the land to the joy of their father; in winter they bear a white shield, but black in summer? Read my, etc.—*Snow-flakes and rain* [the text gives Rep-hens (!)].

21. Who are the maids that go weeping to the joy of their father, white-hooded, fair-haired, wide awake in a gale? Read my, etc.—*The waves.*

22. Who are the maids that go many together to the joy of their father; they have brought grief to many; these goodwives have no husbands? Read my, etc.—*The same.*

23. Who are the brides that walk over the reefs, and drive along the friths; these white-hooded *ladies* have a hard bed; in calm weather they make no stir? Read my, etc.—*The same.*

24. I saw an earth-dweller pass by, a corpse sitting on a corpse: a blind one riding on a blind sea-car, yet the steed was lifeless? Read my, etc.—*A dead horse floated on an icefloe.*

25. What is that beast, all girdled with iron, which kills the flocks; it has eight horns, but no head, and ....? Read my, etc.—*The húnn* (*bear*) *or headpiece in the game of hnef-tafl* (*fox and geese*).

26. What is that beast that shelters the Danes; with bloody back it covers men, encounters spears, saves many a life, fitting its body to the hands of men? Read my, etc.—*The shield.*

27. A .... yearning for children, gathered her building materials, straw-choppers fenced her in, whilst above her was drink's echoing hall. Read my, etc.—*A duck building her nest in a neat's head with the horns on.*

28. Four ganging, four hanging, two showing the way, two keeping the dogs off, one ever dirty lags behind. Read my, etc.—*A cow.*

29. Who is it that sleeps in the hearth, all made of stone,—a mischievous being without father or mother,—there is his lifelong abode? Read my, etc.—*A spark hidden in a flint.*

30. I saw a horse, a maid whipped it, she shook a . . . .? Read my, etc.—*A loom* (the upright) *worked by a woman.*

31. Who are the champions riding to court sixteen together; they send their men far and wide to make settlements? Read my, etc.—*The table (game) of King Itrek.*

32. I saw in summertide a household awake and merry at sunset; the gentlemen drank their beer in silence, but the ale-butt stood and screamed. Read my, etc.—*A sow with a litter of sucking pigs.*

33. I saw certain dust-like maidens; the rocks were their bedding; they are black and swart in sunshine, but the less one can see [i. e. in the dark] the fairer they look. Read my, etc.—*Pale embers on the hearth.*

34. I saw on a (see the text). *A pun,* (a hearth, a hawk, a duck, talons.)

35. Who are the two that have ten feet, three eyes, one tail? Read my, etc.—*The one-eyed Woden riding Sleipni his eight-legged steed.*

36. What did Woden whisper into Balder's ear ere he was borne on the pyre?—*Heidrek cries,* Wonder and wickedness and all sorts of lewdness!

Being vanquished he has now forfeited his life, but he treacherously draws his magic brand Tyrfing and strikes at Woden, who flies away in the shape of a hawk. Heidrek however soon afterwards perishes, slain by his slaves with his own sword.

HARBARDSLJÓD (LAY OF HÁRBARD)

Thor ordinarily spurned marine carriers and waded across rivers and sounds; but on one return journey from a campaign in Giant Land, he came to a body of water that was so deep that his poke of thunderbolts would be quenched if he went through it. The ferryman, **Hárbard** ("Hoar Beard") was Odin in disguise. The two matched wits, and the crafty Odin easily got the better of frank, literal-minded Thor. Odin refused Thor passage, and the latter was compelled to take the long roundabout way back to Asgard. In addition to Odin's exhibition of his wisdom, there are several allusions to myths which will be encountered later. There is a tone of satire which suggests that the poet still believes in the old traditions but has his doubts. It was probably composed in a transitional period when Christianity had made substantial inroads in the north.

SCENE, *on the banks of a river, Thor shouting on the one bank for the ferryman who is on the other.*

Thor. WHO is that lad of lads, that stands across the river?—*H.* Who is that churl of churls, that shouts across the water?—*T.* Ferry me across the water, I will give thee food to-morrow. I have a basket on my back; there was never better meat; I dined, as I rested before I went from home, on herring and goat-venison; I am still sated with it.—*H.* Thou rejoicest in an early meal. Little thou knowest it, but dismal is thy home; I guess thy mother be dead.—*T.* Thou tellest me now, what is the worst news to every man, that my mother is dead.—*H.* It looks little like thy having three estates; there thou art, bare-legged in a beggar's gaberdine; not even thy breeches on.—*T.* Bring the boat here, I will show thee the berths. Who owns the bark thou holdest by the shore?—*H.* Hildwolf is his name, who bade me hold her here; the shrewd husbandman who lives in Radsey Sound. He told me not to ferry over any poachers or horse-thieves, but only good men and such as I knew well. Tell me thy name, if thou wilt cross the Sound.—*T.* I will, though an outlaw, give my name, and all my kin and dwelling. I am Woden's son, Meili's brother, and Main's father, the Strong One of the Gods; it is with Thor thou speakest. Now I will ask what is thy name?—*H.* My name is Hoarbeard; I never hide my name.—*T.* Why shouldst thou hide thy name, unless thou be an outlaw?—*H.* Even though I were an outlaw, I could keep my life safe from such as thee, unless I were death-doomed.—*T.* 'Tis a bad job to have to wade through the water to thee and wet my quiver; I should pay thee, thou quiver-boy (wee boy), for thy mockery, if I were to cross the Sound. —*H.* Here I shall stand, and bide thy coming; thou shalt not have met a better man since Hrungni's death.—*T.* Now thou tellest how Hrungni and I dealt together, that stout-hearted Giant, whose head was of stone; yet I felled him and brought him low. What wast thou doing then?—*H.* I was with Fiolware five winters together on an island called Allgreen; we fought there, and made a slaughter: tried many things, meddled with love.—*T.* What manner of women were those women of yours? —*H.* Sparks of women they were, had they but been wise; fair they were, if they had been but faithful. They wound rope out of sand, and dug down the dales into a field. I got the better of them all. I slept with these seven sisters, took my pleasure with them all. What wert thou doing the while, Thor?

Thor. I smote Thiazi, the mighty Giant; I flung the eyes of Alwald's son up into the clear heaven; these are the greatest tokens of my works, which all men may see hereafter. What wert thou doing the while, Hoarbeard?

H. Many love adventures I had with the night-riders (hags), when I wiled them from their husbands. Sturdy Giant, indeed, was Leebeard; he gave me a magic wand, but I wiled him out of his wit.—*T.* Ill didst thou requite good gift then.—*H.* One oak takes what is scraped from another. Every man for himself. What wast thou doing the while, Thor?

Thor. I was in the east, smiting the ill-working Giant-brides on their way to the hills. Great would be Giant-kind were they all alive. No man could then live on this earth. What wast thou doing the while, Hoarbeard?

H. I was in Welshland, busy a-fighting; I drove kings to fight, but never wrought peace. Woden owns all the gentlefolk that fall in fight, but Thor the thrall-kind.—*T.* Thou wouldst share out unfair odds among the Anses, if the power were thine.

H. Thor has strength enough, but no heart; from fear and cowardice thou wast packed away in a glove, and wast not much like Thor then; thou darest not in thy terror either to sneeze or .... lest Fialar heard it.—*T.* Thou coward, Hoarbeard, I would smite thee to death if I could stretch across the Sound.—*H.* Why stretch across the Sound when there is no cause? What didst thou the while, Thor?

Thor. I was in the East, and defended the river, when Swarang's sons set upon me; they pelted me with stones, yet they did not enjoy victory, they were obliged to beg quarter of me. What wast thou doing the while, Hoarbeard?

H. I was in the East, in adventure with a certain lady; I played with the linen-white one, and held a secret love-meeting; I gladdened the gold-bright lady. She, the maid, enjoyed the sport.—*T.* Ye had a good choice of maidens then.—*H.* I needed thy help then, Thor, that I might keep hold of that linen-white maid.—*T.* I would have helped if I had had the chance.—*H.* I would have trusted thee, if thou hadst not broken truce with me.—*T.* I am no such heel-biter as an old brogue in the spring. —*H.* ..... What wast thou doing the while, Thor?—*T.* I smote the Bearsark brides in Leesey, they had wrought the worst deeds, wiling all people.—*H.* That was a shameful deed of thee, Thor, to beat women.—*T.* She-wolves they were, but hardly women. They shattered my ship which I had beached, threatened me with an iron club, and chased Thialfi. What wast thou doing the while, Hoarbeard?

H. I was in the army, which was marching hither, hoisting the war-banner, and reddening the spear.—*T.* Now thou art telling how thou wentest to do harm to us.—*H.* I will make it good to thee with a hand-ring, as the daysmen order who shall settle our cause.

Thor. Where didst thou learn those cutting words? I never heard words more cutting.—*H.* I learnt them from the old [giantesses] that live in the home-howes.—*T.* Thou givest a (too) fair name to cairns, when thou callest them home-howes.—*H.* So I judge on this head (that is what I call them).—*T.* Thy word-fencing will turn out ill to thee, if I do set myself to wade across; thou wouldst, methinks, cry louder than the Wolf, if thou shouldst get a stroke of the Hammer.—*H.* Sif [thy wife] has a paramour at home, go and seek him, that is a job for thee; 'tis nearer at hand to thee.—*T.* Thou lettest thy tongue lead thee to say what is most offensive to me; thou coward, Hoarbeard, thou liest, I warrant thee.

H. I speak true, I warrant thee; thou art too slow on thy journey. Thou wouldst have been far on thy way now, if thou hadst started at break of day.—*T.* Hoarbeard, thou coward, how long thou hast kept me waiting.—*H.* I never thought a ferryman could stop Anses-Thor's journey.—*T.* I will give thee counsel; pull the boat hither; let us stop hooting. Come to meet Magni's father (me).

H. Get thee gone from the Sound, passage shall be denied thee.—*T.* Then shew me the way, since thou wilt not ferry me across the water. —*H.* That is a small thing to refuse. It is no long way to go; an hour to the stock; an hour to the stone; then keep on to the left hand, till thou comest to Werland, there shall Fiorgyn meet her son; and then she will tell thee the highway to the land of Woden.—*T.* Shall I get there to-day?—*H.* Aye, thou wilt get there with great toil and trouble at sunrise, or nigh about, I think.

Thor. Short shall our talk be, since thou answerest me nothing but mocking. I will pay thee back for refusing me passage, if we two meet again.

H. Get thee gone. May all the fiends take thee!

SKÍRNISMÁL (WORDS OF SKÍRNIR)

This charming romantic poem is the only one in the collection in which Frey plays a significant role. Actually it is an old fertility cult song put in dramatic form. Frey represents the sun god. The name Skírnir may properly be associated with the adjective skírr, "bright." Gerda is connected with the word "gard" or "yard" and possibly symbolizes a grain field held in the grip of frost giants or may be a yonic symbol or both. Gymir is the earth giant. Barra, the grove where the lovers are united, is connected with Old Norse barr and other words meaning "corn" or "barley". It is quite natural that a vernal fertility celebration involving Frey and Gerda should be presented in the dramatic dialog which is the form of this poem. However, the tenderness of the love story is rare in any genre of Old Norse literature.

Skírnir's threat of dire magical curses to Gerda is one of two examples of bonafide imprecation through sorcery in the Poetic Edda. The other is Sigrún's curse in the Helgakvida Hundingsbana II. In addition, such songs are mentioned in the Hávamál and the Sigrdrifomál (commentary under Reginsmál, infra).

Frey paid dearly for his bride: He went to Ragnarǫk without his sword and fell in this ultimate battle with the forces of evil.

FIRST SCENE.—*At Elfham, in Frey's Hall. Skadi, Frey's mother, speaks to Skirni, Frey's messenger.*

Skadi. ARISE, Skirni, and go and get speech of our son, and ask our goodly son with whom he is angry.—*Skirni.* I shall get but evil words from your son if I try to speak with him and ask your goodly son against whom his wrath is kindled.

SECOND SCENE.—*Skirni goes up to Frey.*

Skirni. Tell me, O Frey, thou captain of the Gods, fain would I know why thou, my lord, sittest the livelong day alone in thy hall.—*Frey.* How can I tell thee, my young boy, my heavy heart-sorrow. For the sun shines day by day, but brings no joy to me.—*Skirni.* Can thy grief be so great that thou, my friend, couldst not tell it to me? For we were lads together in past days; well might we two trust one another.— *Frey.* In Gymis' crofts I saw a-walking a maid I love; her arms beamed so that sky and sea were lit thereby. This maid is dearer to me than ever maid was to a young man. But none of the Anses or of the Elves will have us be together.—*Skirni.* Now give me the horse to bear me through the dark flicker-flame thou knowest of; and that sword that fights of itself against the Giant-kind.—*Frey.* I will give thee the horse to bear thee

37

through the dark flicker-flame; and that sword that fights of itself if he is bold that bears it.

THIRD SCENE.—*Skirni on his way talks to his horse.*

Skirni. It is dark all about us, it is time for us to go over the wet hills, over Ogre-land. We shall both get there unless that foul giant takes us both.

FOURTH SCENE.—*In Giant-land, outside Gymis' hall. To the Shepherd.*

Skirni. Tell me, Shepherd, sitting on the howe and watching all the ways, how I may come to talk with the young maid, maugre Gymis' hounds.

Shepherd. Art thou fey, or art thou a ghost?... Thou canst never get to talk with Gymis' goodly maid.—*Skirni.* He must never be flinching whoso wants to go on with his journey. On one day my fate was fashioned and all my life laid down.

FIFTH SCENE.—*Inside the hall. Gerda and a bondsmaid.*

Gerda. What is that clattering clatter that I hear in our court? The earth is quaking, and all Gymis' homestead shaking.—*Bondsmaid.* A man is without here, he has got off his horse, and lets his steed graze.—*Gerda.* Go, bid him in to our hall, to drink of our clear mead; though it misgives me that my brother's slayer is without.

SIXTH SCENE.—*Gerda welcomes Skirni to the hall.*

Gerda. Which of the sons of Anses or of wise Wanes is this? How didst thou alone get over the huge fire to visit our hall?—*Skirni.* I am none of Anses nor of Elves nor of wise Wanes, though alone I came over the huge fire to visit your hall. I have here eleven all-golden apples; these, Gerda, will I give thee to purchase thy favour, that thou mayest call Frey the best-beloved of all living.

Gerda. Thy eleven apples I will never take, for any one's love; nor shall we two, Frey and I, ever live together.—*Skirni.* I will give thee a ring that was burnt with Woden's young son; eight rings as heavy drop therefrom every ninth night.—*Gerda.* I take no ring, even though burnt with Woden's young son. I lack no gold in Gymis' house, sharing my father's wealth.

Skirni (threatening). Look on this blade, maid, slender, marked with characters, that I hold in my hand; I will hew thy head from off thy neck unless thou yieldest to me.—*Gerda.* I shall never bear to be driven to love any man. Yet I guess if thou and Gymir meet, you will come to fight.—*Skirni.* Look at this blade, etc. Before its edge the old giant shall bow down and thy father fall doomed. I shall touch thee with a magic wand, for I will tame thee, maiden, to my will; thou shalt go where the sons of men shall never see thee, on the Eyrie-mound thou shalt for ever sit, looking out of the world, sniffing Hellwards. Meat shall be more loathsome to thee than is the cruel Serpent to any man. Thou shalt be made a show of, when thou comest out. May Rimni (the giant) grin upon thee; may everything stare on thee; thou shalt be better known than the watchman (Heimdall) among the Gods, gaping through the gate! May (the magical characters) Maddener and Whooper, Teasle and Lust, bring upon thee tears and sorrow! Sit thee down, I will yet tell thee a heavy... and double grief. May the demons pinch thee every

38

day in Giant-land; thou shalt creep loveless and lovelorn to the Frost-Giants' hall day by day, thou shalt have weeping for joy, and wear out sorrow with tears. Thou shalt linger for ever with a three-headed monster, or else be husband-less. May thy soul be smitten! May thou pine away with pining! Be thou like a thistle-head thrust away in the porch! I went to the holt, and to the . . . wood to fetch the magic wand, and got it. Woden is wroth with thee, the pride of the Anses (Thor) is wroth with thee; Frey shall hate thee. Thou, most wicked maid, hast brought down upon thee the wrath of the Gods.—Hearken, O Giants! Hearken, ye Frost-Giants! ye sons of Suttung! ye companies of the Anses! how I forbid, how I deny her all joy of men, all pleasure of men. A monster called Rimegrim below Corse-gates shall have thee (to wife). There the sons of toil underneath the roots of the wood shall serve thee with . . . .; no better drink shalt thou get, maid, for thy pleasure, at my pleasure.— I engrave thee with the sign 'Þ' and the three signs, Lewdness, Love-Madness, Lust.—Yet will I scrape it off as I scratched it on, if need be.

Gerda (*cowed, now brings him a goblet*). Hail now, lad, and take this foaming cup full of old mead! Though I had not thought that I should ever love the Waningi (Frey) well.—*Skirni*. I must have a full answer before I ride hence; when wilt thou have a love-tryst with Niord's blooming son?—*Gerda*. Barra is the name of a peaceful copse we both know; there after three nights Gerda will grant her love to Niord's son.

SEVENTH SCENE.—*Skirni back at Elfham telling his success to Frey.*

Frey. Tell me, Skirni, before thou castest saddle off thy horse and takest one step forward, How didst thou fare in Giant-land—for thy pleasure, or mine?—*Skirni*. Barra is the name of a peaceful copse we both know; there after three nights' time Gerda will grant her love to Niord's son.

EIGHTH SCENE.—*Frey (soliloquising).* One night is long, two nights are longer! How can I endure three? A month has often seemed shorter to me that this half (short) bridal night.

HYMISKVIDA (LAY OF HYMIR)

This pleasing little tale describes one of Thor's visits to Gaint Land (cf. also the Harbardsljod, Thrymskvida, Lokasenna, and Snorri's tale of the visit to Utgard-Loki, the latter not in the Poetic Edda). The poem itself is relatively late and may be a conglomerate of two or more traditions, but it is put together skillfully and told with verve and a mild humor. The glimpses of social life and customs in Gaint Land suggest that the domestic life of this race was envisioned as not much different from that of humans and gods. It is possible that the poem was intended for recitation at banquets and drinking bouts.

The Gods are feasting at Eager's. The unwilling host at parting sends Thor on a forlorn errand for a cauldron for future entertainments.

IN days of old the blessed Gods drank together, and gathered at the feast: ere they had their fill, they cast the divining rods, and inspected the blood, finding at Eager's all good cheer.

The simple giant [Eager], like the Mud-monster's son, was sitting; Woden's son [Thor] looked him defiantly in the face, *saying,* 'Thou shalt often make a feast for the Anses!' The taunting wight [Thor] gave the giant trouble; he [Eager] thought to pay out the Gods in his turn. He bade Sif's Husband bring him the cauldron 'wherein I may brew the ale for all of you.' None of blessed Gods, nor of the Powers above, could anywhere get such a cauldron, until Tew secretly gave the Thunderer the best of counsel:—'There lives east of the Sleet-bays, at the ends of heaven, a hundred-wise giant, called Hymi. My grim father owns a mighty cauldron a mile deep.' —*Thor.* 'Thinkest thou we can get this lee-vat.'—*Tew.* 'Yes, friend, if we contrive a plot for it.'

Now they made speed all day long, till they came to Egil's [Tew's uncle]. He stalled the proud-horned goats. Then they wended to the hall that Hymi owned. The grandson [Tew] found his granddam, loathsome to look on, having nine hundred heads. But another came forth, bright as gold, fair-browed, bearing a beer-cup to her son, *saying,* 'Thou child of Giants! I will hide you stout-hearted twain underneath the cauldron. My husband is oftentimes sharp and savage to his guests.'

But now that woe-maker, the sturdy Hymi, came late home from hunting; he walked into the hall; the icicles clattered; the churl's chin-thicket [beard] was frozen. *Giant-wife says:* 'Hail, Hymi! be not angry! thy son is come to thy hall, whom we have been looking for, off a long journey. With him comes the Giant-killer, the friend of man, whose name is Weor [Thor]. Look where they sit under the gable, keeping at safe distance, behind the pillar!'

The giant turns his face towards them. The pillar flew asunder at the look of the giant, and the [cross] beam [*on which the cauldrons lay*] broke in twain. Down came from the shelf eight cauldrons; but one, a hard-wrought one, remained unbroken. Now the two came out, and the old giant fixed his eye on his foeman. It could bode him no good to see him, who makes widows of giantesses, standing on his floor.

Now three steers were taken out, and the giant bade set them to boil. One by one they made them shorter by the head, and set them on the fire. Sif's Husband alone ate, before he slept, three of Hymi's oxen whole. The hoary giant deemed Thor's dinner rather large, *and said :* 'We three shall have to provide some other venison for our supper.'

Next morning Weor [Thor] said he should like to row out fishing, if the bold giant would give bait. *Giant said :* 'Go to the herd, thou Giant-slayer, and get thy bait thyself! I think thou shalt easily find bait from the oxen.' Then the lad [Thor] turned quickly to the wood, where a coal-black ox stood. The Giant-killer wrung the head off the bullock. . . . *Giant said :* 'Thou boatman! thy works are worse than thy sitting still.'

Now they go out fishing.
The Lord of the Goats [Thor] bade the giant pull his boat out further; but the giant said he had no mind to row any longer. The sturdy Hymi kept pulling up whales, two at once, on his hook; while Weor, Woden's kinsman, aft in the boat, was cunningly getting his line ready. He, the Helper of men, the Serpent-slayer, baited his hook with the ox's head. He, the God-abhorred one, that girds all lands round from beneath [the Serpent], gulped down the bait. The doughty Thor pulled amain the venom-streaked Serpent up to the gunwale, and battered with the Hammer the hideous head of the Wolf's twin-brother. The Dragon howled, and the wilderness rang; even the old Earth shuddered all through. Back sank the sea-monster into the deep.

Moody was the giant as they rowed back, so that he never spoke a word; he steered round with his oar on the other tack.

Ashore the Giant says : 'I pray thee, share half the work with me! Either carry the whales up to the court, or house our ship.' The Thunderer stepped forward, caught hold of the bow, swung the wave-steed [ship] up single-handed, with all the bilge, the oars, and the bilge-scoop in her. He carried the giant's craft up to the court, all along through the rock-cauldrons [caves].

Still the stubborn giant challenged Thor's strength, saying, 'Though a man might pull a good oar, he did not call him strong except he could break his cup.'

Hymi gives him the cup. When the Thunderer grasped the [giant's] beaker [*and cast it*], he soon burst the tall shaft [pillar] in twain. From where he sat he dashed it through the pillars; but they bore it back whole to Hymi again, till the giant's fair leman gave him good counsel, which none but she knew: 'Dash it down on Hymi's skull; that sturdy giant's pate is harder than any cup.' Then the hardy Lord of the Goats [Thor] sprang to his feet, putting forth his whole godly strength; the old churl's skull was unbroken, but the wine-vat was cracked all across.

The giant cries, whimpering : 'Many good things have now departed from me, now I see my cup broken at my feet. Now,' the old fellow said, 'I can no more say, "Ale, thou art brewed."'

The giant tells Thor : 'The last Task is, if thou canst carry my ale-cauldron out of my hall.' Tew tried twice to lift it, but each time the cauldron stood still [*he could not stir it*]. Then the Father of Modi [Thor] caught hold of the brim, and his feet sank down through the floor of the hall. Sif's Husband [Thor] clapped the cauldron upon his head [*like a hat*], and the [*pot-hooks*] chains rattled about his heels.

They had not passed far upon their path, when Woden's son [Thor] looked once back; he saw a many-headed throng come from the East, following Hymi from their dens. He [Thor], as he stood, cast the cauldron down from his shoulders, and swung the murderous Miollni before him, and smote all the whales [monsters] of the wilderness.

They had not passed long on their way, when the Thunderer's goat fell down half-dead; the shaker of the car-pole [the goat] was lame on one leg; it was the guileful Loki's doing.

[*The Poet's epilogue*]: Now ye have heard—every mythologist can tell all about it—what pledge he [Thor] exacted from the Giant [Egil], who had to pay him both his children as ransom. So the Mighty One [Thor] came to the assembly of the Gods, bringing the cauldron that Hymi had owned.

[*The Gleeman's epilogue*]: Now Weor [Thor] shall surely drink ale at Eager's, once every harvest-time [*like a harvest-kern*].

THRYMSKVIDA (LAY OF THRYM)

Here we have one of the older poems in the Poetic Edda. From the structural and prosodic standpoints it is a superior work. The presentations of sly, quick-witted Loki and the angry Thor, reluctantly but necessarily assuming the role of a transvestite, are masterful. The importance of Thor's hammer as the principal defense of Asgard is brought out clearly. Nothing else but the need to retrieve it could have persuaded manly Thor to put on woman's clothing.

The passion of the giants for Freya, a fertility goddess, is also a major theme in Snorri's story about the giant mason who built the walls of Asgard and wanted Freya, the sun, and moon as payment (not in the Poetic Edda). Just as we noted in the Hymiskvida, the life of the giants reflects the aristocratic society in the noble halls of the mediaeval Scandinavian nobility, and a gracious lady was needed to preside over them jointly with her master.

WROTH waxed Wing-Thor when he awoke and missed his Hammer; he shook his beard and tossed his locks, the Son of Earth groped about him with his hands, and this was the first word that he spoke: 'Hearken now, O Loki, to what I am telling thee, a thing unheard of either on earth or in the heavens above. Thor has been robbed of his Hammer!'

They went to the fair Freya's bower, and this was the first word that he spoke: 'Wilt thou lend me thy feather-fell, Freya, that I may be able to find my Hammer?'—*Quoth Freya:* 'Yea, I would give it thee though it were of gold, and grant it thee even though it were of silver.'

Then away flew Loki, the feather-fell rattled, till he won out of Ansgard and won into Giant-land. Thrym, the Giants' lord, was sitting on a howe plaiting golden leashes for his grey-hounds, and trimming the manes of his horses; and this was the first word that he spoke: 'How goes it with the Anses? How goes it with the Elves? Why hast thou come alone into Giant-land?'—Quoth Loki, Laufey's son: 'It goes ill with the Anses! It goes ill with the Elves! Hast thou hidden the Thunderer's hammer?'—Quoth Thrym, lord of Giants: 'Yea, I have hidden the Thunderer's hammer eight miles deep under the earth. No man shall ever bring it back, save he bring me Freya to wife.'

Then away flew Loki—the feather-fell rattled—till he won out of Giant-land, and won into Ansgard. Thor met him in the gate, and this was the first word that he spake: 'Hast thou good news for thy toil? Tell me all thy tidings from the sky, for he that speaks sitting down often stumbles in his speech, and he that speaks lying down is often guilty of a lie.'—Quoth Loki, Laufey's son: 'I have good news for my toil. Thrym, the Giant lord, has thy Hammer. No man shall ever bring it back, save he bring him Freya to wife.'

They went to the fair Freya's bower, and this was the first word that he [Thor] spake: 'Take thy bride's veil, Freya, we two must drive to Giant-land.'

Wroth waxed Freya, and snorted with rage; the hall of the Anses shook all over, the great Brising necklace snapped, and this was the first word that she spoke: 'Sure I were proved the man-maddest of women, should I drive with thee to Giant-land.'

At once the Anses all went into council, and all the goddesses into parley; the mighty Gods took counsel together how they might get back the Thunderer's hammer.

Then Heimdall spake, the whitest of the Anses; he had great fore-sight, as all the other Wanes have: 'Let us wrap Thor in the bride's veil, let him have the great Brising necklace, let the bunch of keys rattle down from his girdle, and a woman's coats fall about his knees, and fasten the broad stones [brooches] on his breast, and wind the hood neatly about his head.'

Then up spake Thor, that doughty God: 'Surely the Anses would call me lewd fellow, if I were to let myself be wrapped in a bride's veil.'

Then up spake Loki, Laufey's son: 'Speak not so, O Thor, for the Giants will soon dwell in Ansgard save thou get back thy Hammer.'

Then they wrapped Thor in the bride's veil, and gave him the great Brising necklace, let the keys rattle down from his girdle, and the woman's coats fall about his knees, and fastened the broad stones [brooches] at his breast, and wound the hood neatly about his head.

Then spake Loki, Laufey's son: 'I will follow thee as bridesmaid; we two will drive to Giant-land.'

The goats were fetched out at once, they were harnessed to the car-poles, that they might run swiftly. The rocks were rent, the earth blazed in flame, as Woden's son drove into Giant-land.

Up spake Thrym, the Giant lord: 'Stand up, my giants all, and strew the benches, they are bringing me Freya to wife, the daughter of Niord, of Noatown. There are here in the yard gold-horned kine, and black unspotted oxen, the delight of the Giant lord. I have trea-sures in store, I have jewels in store, I lack nought but Freya.'

Early in the evening the guests gathered, and ale was served to the Giants. Sif's husband [Thor] ate for his share a whole ox, eight salmon, all the dainties cooked for the ladies, and drank three casks of mead.

Up spake Thrym, the Giant lord: 'Was ever a bride so sharply set? I have never seen a bride take such big mouthfuls, nor a maid drink so deep of mead.'

The quick-witted bridesmaid, sitting by, found ready answer to the Giant's speech: 'Freya has not eaten for eight days, so eager was she to be in Giant-land.'

He [Thrym] bent down under the veil, wishing to kiss the bride, but he started back the whole length of the hall. 'Why are Freya's eyes so awful? it seems as if flames were darting from her eyes.'

The quick-witted bridesmaid, sitting by, found ready answer to the

Giant's speech: 'Freya has not slept for eight nights, so eager was she to be in Giant-land.'

In came the Giants' aged sister (mother?) begging boldly for a bridal fee: 'Take the red-rings off thine arm if thou wouldst win my love, my love and all my heart besides!'

Up spake Thrym, the Giant lord: 'Bring in the Hammer to hallow the bride, lay the Miollni on the Maid's lap. Hallow our hands together in wedlock!'

The heart of the Thunderer laughed in his breast when he felt the hard Hammer with his hands. First he slew Thrym, the Giant lord, and then smote the whole race of Giants. He slew the Giants' aged sister (mother?) who had begged a bridal-fee of him; she got a pound instead of pence, and hammer strokes instead of rings.

This is how Woden's son got back his Hammer. (*Minstrel's epilogue.*)

VǪLUNDARKIVDA (LAY OF VǪLUND)

The Germanic composite of Daedalus and Hephaestus is Vǫlund (English Wayland, German Wieland, French Galant in the chansons de geste). The skillful craftsmen who made labyrinths and magnificent jewelry may well come from a common Indo-European tradition. Like Hephaestus, Vǫlund was lame, but from a different cause. Like cuckolded Hephaestus, Vǫlund managed to avenge himself partially by humiliating a woman (in this case, an innocent one). Like Gudrun, he horrified his enemy by making ale cups from the skulls of the latter's sons (cf. the same custom among the Indo—European Scythians, described by Herodotus, IV, 65). Allrune's Egil, the Philoctetes of Germanic antiquity, reappears briefly in the Vilkina Saga (cf. also the legend of Heming in Saxo's story of Palna-toki and the South German Wilhelm Tell story). It is possible that the Vǫlundarkvida is only the first part of a trilogy of which the second and third might have dealt with Egil and Slagfid (of whom no more is known).

FROM the south through Mirkwood, to fulfil their fates, the young fairy maidens flew. The Southern ladies alighted to rest on the Sea-strand, and fell to spinning their goodly linen. First Allrune, Cear's fair daughter, took Egil to her bright bosom. The second, [Herwor] Swanwhite, *kissed* Slagfin. But Lathgund her sister clasped the white neck of Weyland. Seven winters they stayed there in peace, but on the eighth they began to pine, on the ninth they must needs part. The young fairy maidens hastened to Mirkwood to fulfil their fates.

The weather-eyed huntsman and Slagfin and Egil came home from the hunt, and found their house empty. They went in and out and sought around. Egil skated eastwards after Allrune, and Slagfin south-wards after Swanwhite. But Weyland sat alone behind in Wolf-dale, hammering the red gold upon 'the stithy,' closing all the ring-bands tightly. Thus he awaited his bright wife if peradventure she might come.

But Nidad, king of the Niars, heard that Weyland was sitting alone in Wolf-dale. The men marched forth by night, in their studded mail-coats, their shields shining against the waning moon. They alighted from their saddles at the hall gable, and went in forthwith right up the hall. There they saw rings threaded on bast, seven hundred in all, which the hero owned; and they took them off the bast and put them on again, all save one, which they took away. Home from the hunt came the weather-eyed hero Weyland gliding along the far track. He . . . . roasting a she-bear's flesh, high blazed the faggots of rock-dry fir : the wind-dry wood before Weyland. He sat down on the bear-skin, and told his rings over, the Elves' king, but one he missed, and he thought that Lathgund the young fay, Lodwe's daughter, must have come back. He sat so long that at last he fell asleep; but he awoke in helpless plight, he felt the heavy shackles on his hands and the fetters clasped about his feet.

Then spake Weyland, lord of the Elves, 'Who are the heroes that have "handled my rings" and bound me?'

Then shouted Nidad, king of the Niars, 'Where didst thou get such treasures untold in Wolf-dale, O Weyland, lord of the Elves? There was no gold in Glisten-heath, and I thought our land was far from the hills of Rhine.'

Then spake Weyland, lord of the Elves: 'Far more good things had we, I remember, when it was well with us all at home: Lathgund and Herwor, Lodwe's daughters; dear was Allrune, Cear's daughter, to us .... (*Several lines are missing here.*)

They bring Weyland to Nidad's palace and the Queen [Cynwig?] is standing outside: she mocks the prisoner and advises Nidad to hamstring him and set him on an island to work jewels and treasures for him.

Cynwig the queen of Nidad was standing without, she went in up the hall, she stood on the floor and raised her voice: 'He does not look blithe that is coming out of the wood. His eyes are like to the eyes of the flashing snake. He will open his lips *and smile*, when the sword is shown to him, and he perceives Bodwild's ring .... Sever the might of his sinews [hamstring him] and set him down in Sea-stead....'

Then spake Weyland, lord of the Elves: 'Nidad's sword glitters on his girdle, the sword I whetted with all my skill, and tempered with all my cunning. That keen blade is now gone from me for ever. I shall not see it carried to Weyland's smithy. Bodwild is wearing my bride's red ring. I shall never be recompensed ....'

He sat down, nor slept at all, but smote with his hammer; he speedily fashioned a snare for Nidad.

The two young boys, the sons of Nidad, rushed to Wolfmere in Seastead. They came to the chest, called for the keys; their greediness was clear when they looked in. There was abundance of treasure; it seemed to them full of red gold and jewels.

Then spake Weyland, lord of the Elves: 'Come alone, ye two, come to-morrow. I shall make this gold yours. Tell it not to the maidens nor to the hall-servants, nor to any man that ye are coming to me.'

Early on the morrow the one called to the other, brother to brother, 'Let us go see the rings.' They went to the chest, called for the keys; their greediness was clear as they looked therein. He cut off the heads of those urchins, and laid their feet underneath the bellows' pit. But the scull-pans that lay under their scalps he bound round with silver and gave to Nidad. Out of their eyeballs he made gems, which he sent to Cynwig, Nidad's queen. But out of the teeth of the twain he wrought two breast-brooches and sent them to Bodwild .... Then Bodwild began to praise the ring .... she had broken; 'I dare not tell any one save thee alone.' Then spake Weyland, lord of the Elves: 'I will mend the crack in the gold, so that thy father shall think it fairer, and thy mother much better, and thyself likewise.'

47

He gave her the beer-cup, for he was more guileful than she, so that she fell asleep on the settle.

When he had wrought his will, then said Weyland, lord of the Elves, 'Now I have avenged my cruel losses, all save one.' *Then he made him wings to serve in the place of feet that he might escape from Nidad.*

'Well is me,' said Weyland, 'I have now got back my feet, which Nidad's men bereft me of.' Laughing Weyland rose into the air, but Bodwild weeping left the island, in bitter grief for her lover's departure and her father's wrath.

Cynwig, Nidad's queen, was standing without; she went in up the hall. But he alighted down to rest on the wall of the hall. 'Art thou waking, Nidad, king of the Niars?' Then spake Nidad, king of the Niars: 'I am ever waking. I cannot sleep for sorrow ever since my son's death. Thy head is a-chill, thy devices have been cold to me. But now I would fain reason with Weyland. Tell me this, Weyland, lord of the Elves, what became of my brave boys.' Then spake Weyland, lord of the Elves: 'Thou shalt swear full oath to me before I speak, upon the ship's bulwark, and upon the shield's rim, upon the horse's shoulder, and upon the brand's edge, that thou wilt not put my wife to death, nor be the slayer of my bride, even though I have a wife known to thee, or we have a child within thy house. Go to the smithy thou didst set up, thou shalt find the bellows stained with blood. I cut off the heads of thy boys and laid their bodies under the bellows' pit. But their scull-pans that were under their scalps I bound with silver and gave to Nidad, and I made gems out of their eyeballs and sent them to Cynwig, Nidad's queen, and out of the teeth of the twain I wrought two breast-brooches and sent them to Bodwild. Bodwild goes great with child, the only daughter of you both.'

Then spake Nidad, king of the Niars: 'Thou never spakest word which grieved me more, nor that I could blame thee more for, Weyland! There is no man here that can reach thee from horseback, nor so strong that he could shoot thee from below when thou soarest up there against the clouds.'

Laughing Weyland rose into the air, but Nidad sat behind in sorrowful mood. Then spake Nidad, lord of the Niars: 'Rise up, Thankred, thou best of my thralls, bid Bodwild, the white-browed fair-clad maiden, to come and speak to her father.' Then said Nidad, lord of the Niars: 'Is it true, Bodwild, that which is told me, did ye sit together, thou and Weyland, in the island?' Then said Bodwild: 'That which is told thee, Nidad, is true; I sat with Weyland in the island a little hour; would I never had. I could not prevail against him, I might not prevail against him.'

LOKASENNA (THE FLYTING OF LOKI)

Loki has no exact parallel in other mythologies. He is a combination of Lucifer (with whose Latin name, from lux, "light," Loki's name may be cognate), Judas Ischariot, and the late and unlamented Vidkun Quisling. He is handsome, quick-witted, often charming, and sworn by a blood ritual to brotherhood with Odin (the explanation of how evil can exist in Asgard). He helped the gods, but often the difficulties from which he extricated them were generated by himself. Snorri, who was apparently fascinated by the sinister character of Loki, related the full biography from his genealogy to his death at Ragnarǫk.

Loki's terrible brood out of the giantess Angerboda showed the bad blood. There was Fenris-Wolf, the horrid creature who had to be put in the bonds of a magic chain which was rent asunder only at Ragnarǫk; Joermungand (the World Serpent, or Midgard Serpent), hooked and nearly landed by Thor on the fishing trip with Hymir; and vile Hel, ruler of the underworld, not a gentle Persephone but more like the repulsive Hecate. Loki also had another mate, the loyal Sigyn. The scene of Loki's flyting was the last banquet of the gods, just after the death of Balder. Aegir, or Gymir, a marine deity, was the host, and ale was served by his two ingratiating servants, Fimafeng and Eldir, from the great crock brought back by Thor from Hymir's stronghold. Loki could not bear to hear the praise of Fimafeng and slew him. He was chased into the forest, but he returned and began his insolent talk that is contained in this poem. There are many obscure allusions not found elsewhere, possibly legacies from Indo-European antiquity.

Again driven from the hall, Loki was pursued to the mountains where he was bound with the entrails of his son out of Sigyn, Nari. Over him were fettered two poisonous serpents whose venom dripped on his head. Sigyn caught the poison in a dish; but whenever she turned to empty it, the continued trickling fell on Loki's face and and indúced spasms violent enough to cause earthquakes (an etio—logical story). Loki's place of bondage may also have been envisioned as the bottom of a volcano such as Hekla.

FIRST SCENE, *in Eager's Hall (Okeanos); all the Gods and Goddesses, save Thor, present at a banquet. Loki appears at the door.*

Loki at the door to Eldi the Cook. Tell me, Eldi (*Cook*), before thou goest further, what the Blessed Gods talk of over their Ale!—*Eldi.* The Blessed Gods are comparing their weapons and their exploits. Of all the

Anses and Elves within, not one speaks a good word for thee.—*Loki*.
I shall go into Eager's hall, to see this banquet; I will bring the Gods
bitter spice for their drink, and mix their mead with venom.—*Eldi*.
Be sure, if thou goest in to behold the banquet, and pourest foul words
and filthy slander on the bounteous Gods, that they will wipe it off on
thee.—*Loki*. Be sure, Eldi, if we two be left alone to bandy cutting
words, that I shall not lack an answer, if thou speakest too much.

SECOND SCENE.—*Loki enters the Hall.*

Loki. Thirsty, I, Loki, came to this hall off a long journey, to beg
the Anses to give me but one draught of the goodly mead.—(*No answer.*)
Why sit ye so silent, ye moody Gods, speaking no word? Give me seat
and place at this banquet, or else bid me go hence.

Bragi. The Anses will never give thee seat or place at their banquet:
for the Anses know well who deserve the joy of the feast.

Loki and Woden. *Loki*. Dost thou remember, Woden, how we two
in days of old blended blood together? Thou sworest never to taste
ale unless we drank together.—*W*. Get up then, Widar, and let the Wolf's
father (Loki) sit down to the banquet; that Loki may not make mock
of us here in Eager's hall. (*Loki sits down and drinks health to the Gods.*)

Loki and Bragi. *L*. Hail, Anses, hail, Ansesses, and all ye most
holy Gods, except that one Anse, Bragi by name, who sits on the
inner bench.—*B*. I will give thee out of my store a steed and a sword,
moreover Bragi will recompense thee with rings; so thou do not abuse
the Anses. Do not rouse the Gods to anger against thee!—*L*. Thou
hast never had a horse or arm-rings; of all the Anses that are here
to-day thou art the wariest in fight, and the shyest of shooting.—*B*.
Be sure, if I were without Eager's hall, as I am now within it, I would
bear thy head in my hand; and give thee that for thy lies.—*L*. Thou
wilt not do so. Thou art bold enough in thy seat, O Bragi, thou bench-
boaster. Go fight if thou be wroth; a valiant man flinches for nought.

Idun and Loki. *Idun*. I pray thee, Bragi, for our children's sake, and
all our beloved, do not provoke Loki here in Eager's hall.—*L*. Hold thy
peace, Idun; I call thee the lewdest of women, since thou laidest thine
arms, washed white in the water, about thy brother's slayer.—*I*. I am
not provoking Loki in Eager's hall; I am but quieting the beer-stirred
Bragi; I would not see you come to blows in anger.

Gefion and Loki. *G*. Why should ye two Anses bandy angry words
here within? Loki knows . . . .—*L*. Hold thy peace, Gefion! I will now
tell how the fair swain, who gave thee the raiment, and who lay with
thee, stole thy love.

Woden and Loki. *W*. Drunk art thou, Loki, and out of thy wits,
to make an enemy of Gefion; for she knows, as well as myself, the
fate of all men.—*L*. Hold thy peace, Woden, thou never couldst deal
victory fairly out to men; thou often hast given the victory to them
to whom thou shouldst not have given it, to the cowardly.—*W*. Know
that if I gave the victory to whom I should not, to the cowardly, that
thou wast eight winters underneath the earth, a woman, and a milk-
maid; and thou hast borne children, and I call that the part of a . . . .
—*L*. But thou, they say, didst work sorcery in Sams-ey; and thou

50

dealtest in magic, like wise women. In a wizard's shape thou flewest over the earth, and that I call the part of a . . . .

Frigg and Loki. **F.** Ye should never talk of your old doings before men, of what ye two Anses went through in old times. Men should let bygones be bygones.—**L.** Hold thy peace, Frigg; thou art Fiorgyns' daughter, and hast always been wanton; since thou, Woden's wife, laidest We and Wili, thy husband's brothers, both in thy bosom.—**F.** Be sure, if I had here in Eager's hall a son like Balder, thou shouldst never come out alive from the Anses, but thou shouldst be slain in thy anger.—**L.** Willest thou, Frigg, that I tell more of my abominations? It is my doing that thou seest no more Balder ride into the hall.

Freyja and Loki. **F.** Drunk art thou, Loki, telling all your horrors. I ween Frigg knows the fate of all men, though she say it not.—**L.** Hold thy peace, Freyja; I know thee well enough; there is no lack of lewdness in thee; of all Anses and Elves that are here, every one has been thy paramour.—**F.** Loose is thy tongue; it will, I guess, talk down evil on thee. The Gods are wroth with thee, the Ansesses are wroth with thee; thou wilt go home a sadder man.—**L.** Hold thy peace, Freyja; thou art a witch-hag, most full of evil, since thou 'bewitchedst' . . . . and then, Freyja, thou didst . . . .

Niord and Loki. **N.** 'Tis no great matter, though women find them lovers, this man or that man. But it is monstrous that a vile Anse, who has borne children, should have dared to come in here.—**L.** Hold thy peace, Niord; thou wast sent from the east a hostage to the Gods; the maids of Hymi used thee for a . . . . and . . . .—**N.** This is my comfort, though I was sent as a hostage among the Gods from afar, that I have begot a son whom no one hates, and who is best of the Anses.—**L.** Stay now, Niord, keep within measure; I shall not hide it longer; this son thou didst beget with thy sister; that outdoes all.

Ty and Loki. **L.** Frey is the best of all charioteers in Anse-town; he never makes a maid or man's wife weep, and redeems all from their bonds.—**L.** Hold thy peace, Ty, thou couldst never set goodwill between two men. Now I will call to mind that right hand of thine which Fenri bit off thee.—**Ty.** I lack a hand, but thou hast lost thy son the Wolf. Both fare badly. The wolf is in ill plight, for he must wait in bonds for the Doom of the Powers.—**L.** Hold thy peace, Ty. It happened to thy wife to have a child by me. Thou hast never had an ell or a penny for thy damages, thou sorry fellow.

Frey and Loki. **F.** I see the Wolf lying in the mouth of the river till the world falls in ruins. Thy turn will come next to be bound, thou worker of evil, save thou holdest thy peace.—**L.** Thou boughtest Gymi's daughter with gold, and gavest thy sword for her. And when Muspells' sons ride over Murkwood, thou shalt not know with what to fight, thou sorry fellow.

Byggvi (Barleycorn) and Loki. **B.** Be sure, if I had a heritage like Frey the Ingowin and such a seemly seat, I would pound thee to marrow, thou ill-omened crow, and maul thine every limb.—**L.** What is the tiny thing I see there wagging its tail, snuffling about (doglike)? Thou wilt be always at Frey's hearth, yapping at the quern.—**B.** My name is Barleycorn; Gods and men know I am hot-tempered; I am

51

here in high spirits because all Hropt's sons (Anses) are here drinking together.—*L.* Hold thy peace, Barleycorn; thou hast never shared food fairly among men. Hid in the bedstraw, thou wast not to be found when men were a-fighting.

Heimdal and Loki. H. Drunk art thou, Loki, and out of thy wits; why dost thou not . . . .? Too deep drinking makes men babble they know not what.—*L.* Hold thy peace, Heimdal! A dull life was meted out to thee in old times. Thou must ever stand with a wet back, and wake as the Gods' watchman.

Skadi and Loki. S. Thou art easy now, Loki, but thou shalt not long go tail-awag; for the Gods shall bind thee on swords with the guts of thy rime-cold son.—*L.* Be sure, if the Gods, etc. I was the first and the foremost at the slaughter, when we handled Thiazi (thy father) roughly. —*S.* Be sure, if thou wast the first, etc. From my hearth and home there shall ever come cold counsels for thee.—*L.* Thou wast softer of speech to Laufey's son (me), when thou didst bid me to thy bed. We must speak of the . . . .

Sif and Loki. Sif (handing him a goblet). Now hail to thee, Loki, and take this foam-brimmed cup full of old mead, so that thou let but her among the Anses be unreviled.—*Loki (emptying the goblet).* But thou too, if so it be, art a wife who has played thy husband false. I know for sure one rival of the Thunderer (Thor)—no one else but cunning Loki (myself).

Beyla (housewife) and Loki. B. The mountains are a-quaking; the Thunderer must be astir from home; he will quiet those that revile Gods and men here.—*L.* Hold thy peace, Beyla, thou art Barleycorn's wife, and full of malice; nothing more noisome has come among the Anses; thou art altogether filthy, thou serving-woman.

(Here Thor comes in.)

Thor. Hold thy peace, vile being; Miollni, my mighty hammer, shall cut thy speech short. I will knock thy shoulder-knob (head) off, and then thy life is done.—*L.* Ha! here is Earth's son at last; why talkest thou big, Thor? Thou wilt not be so valiant in thy fight with the Wolf, who shall swallow up the Blissful Father (Woden).—*T.* Hold thy peace, Loki, etc. I will fling thee up into the east, where none shall see thee more.—*L.* Never speak to men about thy eastern journeys, since thou, the Hero, didst crouch in a glove-thumb, remembering not that thou wast Thor.—*T.* Hold thy peace, Loki, etc. My right hand will smite thee with the killer of Rungni (Hammer), so that thy every bone shall be broken.—*L.* I mean to live a long life, though thou threatenest me with thy hammer. Skrimnis' straps were too tight for thee, thou couldst not get to thy food, and wast well-nigh starved for hunger.—*T.* Hold thy peace, Loki, etc. The killer of Hrungni shall strike thee dead, and (send thee) down underneath the gates of the Dead.—*L.* I chanted to the Anses, I chanted to the sons of Anses, what the mind bid me; but for thee alone I will go away, for I know thou wilt smite.

Loki (in parting, addresses Eager the host). Thou didst brew thy ale [for a feast], Eager, but thou shalt never more give a banquet. All thy goods here within the flame shall lick, and burn thy back to boot.

BALDRS DRAUMAR (BALDER'S DREAMS)

The most vicious act of Loki, the real cause of his bondage, was the slaying of Balder. For the full story we must again depend on Snorri. After Odin discovered that Balder's life was in danger, Frigg exacted an oath from all things not to harm Balder. The sole exception was the weak and apparently harmless mistletoe. Thus the gods could use him as a target for practice with all manner of weaponry. Note that the concept of invulnerability haunts the mythologies of nearly all peoples (cf. Achilles, Caenis, and Siegfried in the Nibelungenlied).

Loki, who knew the secret of the mistletoe, inveigled blind Hod into casting a dart with a mistletoe warhead at Balder, and the latter fell immediately. Snorri's account of the last rites are reminiscent of the funerals of viking chieftans. Hermod was sent to Hel to fetch back Balder, and he was promised his return on the condition that all things weep for the dead god. Only a giantess named Thok, actually Loki in disguise, refused to mourn, and Balder was lost to Hel for all time. Note that the idea of a visit to the nether world by mortals, gods, or demigods is not unknown to other cultures (cf. Orpheus, Heracles, Aeneas, and Christ's Harrowing of Hell).

. . . . . AT once the Anses all went into council, and all the goddesses to a parley. The mighty gods took counsel together that they might find out why dreams of evil haunted Balder. . . . .

Then Woden arose, the ancient Sire, and laid the saddle upon Sleipni's back. Away he rode down toward Mist-Hell's abode, and there met him a whelp (Hell hound) coming out of a cave; there was blood on its breast, as it ran by the way baying at the Father of Spells. On Woden rode, while the vault rang till he came to the lofty hall of Hell. Then Woden rode to its eastern gate, where he knew the Sibyl's barrow stood. He fell to chanting the mighty spells that move the Dead, till she rose all unwilling, and her corpse spake :—

Sibyl. What mortal is it, whom I know not, that hath put me to this weary journey? I have been snowed on with the snow, I have been beaten with the rain, I have been drenched with the dew, long have I been dead.

Woden. Way-wise is my name, I am the son of War-wise. Tell me the tidings of Hell, and I will tell thee tidings of Earth. For whom are the benches strewn with 'mail-coats,' and the hall so fairly hung with painted shields?

Sibyl. For Balder the mead stands ready brewed, the walls decked with shields, while the sons of the Anses are in merry mood. All unwilling have I spoken ; I will speak no more.

53

Woden. Speak on, O Sibyl; I must enquire of thee till I know all. Next I must know, Who shall be the death of Balder and take the life of Woden's son?

Sibyl. Lo, Hod is bearing a tall branch of fate. He shall be the death of Balder, and take the life of Woden's son. All unwilling have I spoken; I will speak no more.

Woden. Speak on, O Sibyl; I must enquire of thee till I know all. Next I must know, Who shall wreak vengeance on Hod, and lift the slayer of Balder on to the funeral fire?

Sibyl. In the Halls of the West Wrind shall bear a son, Wali, that shall avenge Woden's son when but one night old. He shall neither wash his hands nor comb his hair till he has borne the murderer of Balder to the funeral fire. All unwilling have I spoken; I will speak no more.

Woden. Speak on, O Sibyl; I must enquire of thee till I know all. Next I must know, Who are the maidens that stand weeping to their mind's liking, casting their neck-veils up towards the heavens?

Sibyl. No Way-wise art thou, as I took thee to be, but thou art Woden, the ancient Sire.

Woden. No Sibyl art thou, nor wise woman, but thou art the mother of three Monsters.

Sibyl. Ride homeward, Woden, and glorify thyself, for no other man shall behold me again until Loki breaks loose from his bonds, and the Destroyers come at the Doom of the Powers.

THE WAKING OF ANGANTYR

Like the riddles of Gestumblindi and Svipdagsmál, this poem is not in the Eddic corpus. It is preserved in the Hervarar Saga. The action developes around a fateful weapon (not uncommon in Germanic and other mythologies), the sword Tyrfing. Stolen from its dwarf manufacturers, it was cursed so that it would always bring death to its bearer, that wounds it caused would never heal. Arngrim won the sword in battle and gave it to Angantyr, eldest of his twelve sons. All were slain on the island of Samsey and put to rest (hopefully) in a single barrow. When Hervor, Angantyr's posthumous daughter, learned the name of her father and his fate, she decided to acquire Tyrfing. Knowing is fateful characteristics, the wraith was reluctant to surrender the sword to his daughter.

AT sunset in Munarvoe [Love-bay] the young maid met a man driving his flock home.—*Quoth the Shepherd :* Who comes alone to this island? Begone forthwith and seek guesting [for the night]. *With that he turned to go on his way.—Quoth Herwor :* I shall not seek guesting for the night, for I know none of the island folk. Tell me straightway, ere thou go hence, where are the howes called Hiorward's howes?—*Quoth the Shepherd :* Ask me not that, thou art not wise, thou friend of the wickings, thou art in evil straits. Let us *rather* run as fast as our feet can carry us, for out of doors all is awesome for men to look on. —*Quoth Herwor :* I offer thee a neck-ring as payment for thy guiding. I, the friend of heroes, am not lightly to be stayed.—*Quoth the Shepherd :* No man shall give me such beautiful jewels or fair rings, as shall prevent me from going home. Foolish I hold him that will come hither alone in the dark night: fires are flitting, grave-mounds are opening, field and fen are ablaze. Let us run harder.—*Quoth Herwor :* Let us not be frightened by such snortings [of the flame], though fires be ablaze all over the island. We must not let the ghosts of the dead scare us so quickly. We must parley awhile together.

With that the shepherd sped fast to the woods, away from the voice of the maid, but in this strait the hard-knit heart rose higher in the breast of Herwor.

II.

Herwor goes on alone to where she sees the flames blazing around the Howes, and calls upon the spirits of her father Angantheow and his brethren :—

Awake, O Angantheow! It is Herwor, the only daughter of Tofa and thee, that bids thee awaken! Give me out of the howe the sharp blade which the Dwarves forged for Swafurlami. O Herward, O Hiorward, O Rani, O Angantheow! I bid you all awaken *where ye lie* under the roots of the trees, with helm and with mail-coat, with sharp sword, with shield, and with harness and with reddened spear! (*No answer.*) Surely ye are turned to heaps of dust, ye sons of Arngrim, since no one of the children of Eyfora will speak with me here in Munarvoe. O Herward, O Hiorward, O Rani, O Angantheow! May it be with all of you within your ribs, as if ye were nested in an ant-hill, unless ye give me the sword that Dwale forged. It ill beseems ghosts to keep costly weapons in hiding.

Quoth Angantheow (*answering her out of the howe*) : Herwor, my daughter, why art thou crying out *upon us* words so full of cursing? Thou art walking to thine own destruction, thou art become mad or distraught of wit, bewildered in thy mind, that thou awakenest the dead. Young maid, thou art surely not like other mortals, that thou roamest about the howes by night, and standest before the door of the howe with graven spear and the ore of the Goths, with helmet and with mail-coat.—*Quoth Herwor :* I was aye held to be a mortal, till I came hither seeking your abode. Give me the sharp blade that the Dwarves smithied out of the cairn. It avails thee nought to hide it.—*Quoth Angantheow :* Neither father nor son buried me, nor any others of my kin, *but it was my foemen that laid me in my cairn;* they, the only two that remained alive, got possession of Tyrfing, but afterward one only became the owner thereof.—*Quoth H.* Tell me naught but truth. May the [fiend] only let thee rest whole in thy howe if thou have not Tyrfing with thee. Thou art loth to deal thine only child her heritage!

Quoth A. The gates of Hell are ajar, the howes are opening, the whole round of the island is ablaze before thine eyes. Everywhere out of doors it is an awful sight to see. Haste thee back to thy ships, if thou mayest, maiden!—*Quoth H.* Ye can light no such bale-fire by night as that ye could affright me with the flame thereof. Thy daughter's heart will never quake, yea, though she see a ghost standing at the door of the howe! . . . .

Quoth H. I bind you all with spells, ye dead, that ye may all lie dead and rotten among the ghosts in the grave. O Angantheow, give me the mail-scathing slayer of Hialmar out of the howe!

Quoth A. The slayer of Hialmar lies under my shoulders. It is all wrapped about with fire. I know no maid upon earth that dare take this brand in her hands.—*Quoth H.* I will hold the keen blade and take it in my hands, if I may get it. I care not for the burning fire, the flame sinks before my eyes.—*Quoth A.* Thou art foolish, O Herwor the brave, to rush open-eyed into the fire! I will rather give thee the sword out of the howe, for I cannot deny thee, thou young maiden. [*Here Angantheow hands out the sword and Herwor takes it.*]

Quoth H. Thou hast done well, thou son of the wickings, to give me the sword out of the howe. I hold myself happier in having it, O king, than if I were the conqueror of all Norway.—*Quoth A.* Thou little knowest, my daughter, at what thou rejoicest; hapless are thy words, thou foolish woman. This Tyrfing, if thou wilt believe me, shall be

56

the destruction of all thy race. Thou shalt bear a son, who shall wield Tyrfing in days to come, trusting in his might. Men shall call him Heidrek, he shall be the mightiest man born under the pavilion of the sun . . . .

Quoth H. I must go to my steeds of the billows [ships], the king's daughter is in good heart. I care little, O son of kings, how my sons may hereafter come to quarrel.—*Quoth A.* Thou shalt own it, and enjoy it long; but keep it aye sheathed, this slayer of Hialmar; touch not the edges, there is poison on both of them; this Doomer of men is worse than a plague. Farewell, my daughter, fain would I give thee, if thou wilt believe me, the life of us twelve men, all the goodly strength and pith that the sons of Arngrim lost when they died.

Quoth H. Hail all ye that dwell in the howe! I yearn to be away. I must hasten hence.—*To herself as she turns away and the fires sink and darkness falls again over all:* Surely I felt between Life and Death when the fires were burning all about me! . . . .

GROTTASǪNGR (THE MILL SONG)

Snorri, who knew this entire poem and quoted it in his Edda, provided the most concise and best informed commentary on it (Rasmus Anderson's translation):

Odin had a son by name Skjold, from whom the Skjoldungs are descended. He had his throne and ruled in the lands that are now called Denmark, but were then called Gotland. Skjold had a son by name Fridleif, who ruled the lands after him. Fridleif's son was Frode. He took the kingdom after his father, at the time when the Emperor Augustus established peace in all the earth and Christ was born. But Frode being the mightiest king in the northlands, this peace was attributed to him by all who spoke the Danish tongue, and the Norsemen called it the peace of Frode. No man injured the other, even though he might meet, loose or in chains, his father's or brother's bane. There was no thief or robber, so that a gold ring would be a long time on Jalanger's heath. King Frode sent messengers to Svithjod, to the king whose name was Fjolner, and brought there two maid-servants, whose names were Fenja and Menja. They were large and strong. About this time were found in Denmark two millstones, so large that no one had the strength to turn them. But the nature belonged to these mill-stones that they ground whatever was demanded of them by the miller. The name of this mill was Grotte. But the man to whom King Frode gave the mill was called Hengekjapt. King Frode had the maid-servants led to the mill, and requested them to grind for him gold and peace, and Frode's happiness. Then he gave them no longer time to rest or sleep than while the cuckoo was silent or while they sang a song. It is said that they sang the song called the Grottesong, and before they ended it they ground out a host against Frode; so that on the same night there came the sea-king, whose name was Mysing, and slew Frode and took a large amount of booty. Therewith Frode-peace ended. Mysing took with him Grotte, and also Fenja and Menja, and bade them grind salt, and in the middle of the night they asked Mysing whether he did not have salt enough. He bade them grind more. They ground only a short time longer before the ship sank. But in the ocean arose a whirlpool (Maelstrom, mill-stream) in the place where the sea runs into the mill-eye. Thus the sea became salt.

Two seeresses are come to the king's house, Fenia and Menia; these mighty maids are held in bondage at the palace of Frodi, the son of Fridleif. They were led to the bin, and set to turn the gritstone of the mill .... He [Frodi] bade them take neither rest nor pastime, he must always hear the song of the bondmaids .... They [kept up the never-ceasing song to the thud] .... 'Let us fit the bin, let us lighten the stones.' He [the King] bade the maidens to grind on.

They sang and they whirled the spinning stones, till Frodi's household all fell asleep. Then quoth Menia, as she stood at the mill, 'Let us grind Frodi wealth, let us grind him fulfilment of joy, abundance of riches on the bin of bliss. May he sit on riches; may he sleep on down; may his waking be happy! It were well-ground then. No man shall harm his neighbour, devise any evil, or prepare any slaughter, nor smite with whetted sword, yea, not though he find his brother's slayer bound before him.'

But still his [the King's] word was never other than 'Sleep ye no longer than the cuckoo song stays, or than I can say a single stave!' ....

They fall to grinding again in anger, and this time they mean to grind curses on Frodi and his house. When all were asleep, the one says to the other, as she lets the handle go for a moment—

The hand shall have rest, and the stone shall stand still. I have ground to my mind's liking.

Soon our hands shall take no more rest, till Frodi himself shall say that we have ground it out. The hands shall handle the hard shafts, the gory weapons of war. Waken, Frodi! waken, Frodi! if thou wilt listen to our songs and our stories of old.

Frodi, thou gossip of men, wert no wise man when thou boughtest thy bondmaids. Thou didst choose by strength and appearance, without asking of their race. Hrungni and his father were sturdy, yet Thiazi was mightier still, *and* Idi and Aurnir, our ancestors, from whom we brides of Mountain-giants are sprung. Never had this mill come out of the grit mount, nor the massy millstone out of the earth, nor were the Mountain-giants' maids thus grinding here, if ....

We two playmates were brought up under the earth for nine winters. We busied ourselves with mighty feats; we hurled the cleft rocks out of their places, we rolled the boulders over the giants' court, so that the earth shook withal. We hurled the stones so fast that the massy rocks were split in twain. Afterwards we two seeresses stepped into the array of battle in Sweden, we rent the mailcoats, we hewed the shields, we drove through the gray-clad ranks. We pulled down one king, we set up another; we gave help to the good Gothworm, we never rested till Knui fell. We held this life for a season; we were dear to champions; we gashed the blood out of the wounds with our sharp spears and reddened swords.

But now we are come to the king's hall, unmercifully treated and held in bondage, the mud eating our feet and the chill our heads. We are grinding the Quern of Peace. It is dismal here at Frodi's!

[*Then prophesying the evils to come.*]

'I behold fire burning from the east of the stronghold, the tokens of war are waking, the beacons are kindled. On a sudden a host shall come hither, and burn the hall over the king's head. Thou shalt not hold the Throne of Lethra, the red rings, or the Holy Stones [altars] . . . . .

'Let us grasp the handles harder still, we are . . . . . with gore. My father's maiden [my mother] ground amain because she beheld the doom of a multitude of men . . . . .

'Let us grind on! Yrsa's child [Rolf Kraki] shall avenge Halfdan's death on Frodi. He [Rolf] shall be called her son and her brother. Both of us know that this shall be.'

The maids ground on, putting forth all their strength, the young maids were in giant-fury. The huge props flew off the bin [the iron rivets] . . . . . . The shaft-tree shivered, the bin shot down, the massy mill-stone rent in twain.

But the Mountain-giants' bride spake this word: We have ground, O Frodi, to our mind's liking. We have stood full long at the mill.

THE HELGI TRILOGY
HELGAKVIDA HUNDINGSBANE IN FYRRI
(THE FIRST LAY OF HELGI HUNDING'S BANE)
HELGAKVIDA HJORVARDSSONAR
(THE LAY OF HELGI HJORVARD'S SON)
HELGAKVIDA HUNDINGSBANA QNNOR
(THE SECOND LAY OF HELGI HUNDING'S BANE)

The various traditions in this trilogy are rather confused. The essential plot is that of the hero who won the love of a valkyrie but died at the peak of his fame. She followed him to the grave, and they were reincarnated under new names and went through the same cycle of events with some variation (see prose note, omitted here, at the end of the Helgakvida Hjorvardssonar, "It is said of Helgi and Svava that they were born again," perhaps an attempt to identify the older Helgi story with that of Helgi of the Volsungs).

There is a resumé of the three parts as we have them here in Vigfusson and Powell, I, 130. Munch, pp. 147-168, rearranges the sequence and pulls in other traditions to present the trilogy as a sort of a prologue to the Volsunga Saga (after all, Sigurd was the son of Sigmund and Hjordis, daughter of Eylimi). Some further membra disjecta of the tradition are found in the late and rather inferior saga of Romund Greipsson (see Munch, pp. 242-245, for resumé).

Helgi was not a historical personage, although a few scraps of history occasionally turn up in the Poetic Edda. Rather he was a figure from myth. It is likely that the whole group of poems goes back to an initiation ritual with attendant legend. The poems are hardly a genuine piece of heroic tradition, for the tragic pathos of the typical Germanic hero is lacking. Rather we have here the rousing tale of a victorious chieftan and his romantic love affair.

It is of some interest to speculate on the dates of composition of the three poems, all probably relatively late and after the introduction of Christianity. The first Helgi Lay is probably from the latter part of the eleventh century, while the other two are most likely a century or more younger -- after the establishment of Christianity in the north.

HELGI AND SIGRUN

I. IT was in the olden days, the eagles were screaming, the holy streams were flowing from the Hills of Heaven, when Helgi the stout of heart was born of Borghild, in Braeholt. Night lay over the house when the Fates came to forecast the hero's life. They said that he should be called the most famous of kings and the best among princes. With power they twisted the strands of fate for Borghild's son in Braeholt, they spread the woof of gold and made it fast under the midst of the moon's hall. In the east and in the west they hid the thrums, all the land between was to be his. Neri's sister fastened one strand in the sides of the North, and prayed that it might hold for ever.

There was one thing only that threatened the son of the Wolfings and the lady that bore the darling . . . .

Quoth a raven to a raven, as he sat on a lofty branch, famished for food, 'Somewhat of tidings I know. The son of Sigmund, one night old, stands in his armour—now the day is a-dawning—his eyes flashing like a hero's; friend of the wolves is he. Let us be of good cheer !'

The household looked on him as a dayling [bright son of light], saying, 'Now are good seasons come among men.' The king himself came off the battle-field bearing a fair leek to the young prince. He gave him the name of Helgi with Ringstead, Sunfell, Snowfell, Sigarsfield, Ringhaven, Hightown and Heavening; moreover he gave Sinfiotli's brother an inwrought blood-serpent [sword].

The high-born elm [hero] grew up fair and lovely before his kinsman's eyes, he dealt out the gold and bestowed it on the household, never sparing the red hoards. He did not wait long for a war . . . . When he was fifteen years old he slew the stark Hunding, who had long borne rule over his lands and people. Then the sons of Hunding summoned the child of Sigmund to give them riches and rings, for they had to make him repay them for their father's death and a vast plunder. But the prince paid the heirs neither recompense nor weregild, but bade them await the fierce tempest of spears and the anger of Woden. The king's sons came to the sword-tryst at Lowefell, as was appointed. Frodi's peace was broken between the foes, Woden's greedy hounds ravined over the island. When he had slain the sons of Hunding, Alf and Eywulf, Hiorward and Haward, and destroyed the whole race of Geir-Mimi, the prince sat down beneath the Eagle-Rock. Then over Lowefell there burst flashes of light, and out of the flashes the lightnings leapt . . . . Then appeared high in air a troop of fairies, riding in the field of Heaven; they wore helmets, and their mail-coats were flecked with blood, and from their spear-points light-beams shone. It was early when the king called out of Wolfwood to the Maids of the South and asked them if they would follow him home that night—there was a clang of bowstrings. But Hogni's daughter answered from where she sat on her steed—the shield-clash lulled—'Other matters have we on hand, I ween, than to birl at the ale with the prince [you]. My father has plighted his daughter to the grim son of Granmar, though I, O Helgi, have said that I held King Hodbrord no better than a cat's son. Yet he will come, within a few days' space, save thou, O prince, challenge him to battle or deliver me out of his hand.' 'Fear not, maiden, the slayer of Isung [Hodbrord], there shall be a rattle of blades first, unless I be dead.'

Thence the king sent messengers over land and sea to call out a levy, promising the warriors and their sons gold in good store. 'Bid them get aboard their ships forthwith and make ready to sail from Brandey.' There the prince waited, till there came thither warriors by hundreds from Hedinsey. Forthwith the gold-decked fleet stood out to sea from Staffness. Then quoth Helgi to Hiorleif, 'Hast thou mustered the blameless host?' And the young king answered that it were long to tell over the high-stemmed ships freighted with mariners from Crane-ore, as they sailed out to sea down Yorwa-sound, twelve hundred trusty men. 'Yet there lies at Hightown a king's host twice as great. We must make us ready for battle.'

The host awoke, they could see the brow of dawn; the king bade furl the bow-awnings, and they hoisted the woven canvas to the yards in Warinsfirth. Then there arose a plashing of oars and a rattle of iron, shield clashed against shield as the Wickings rowed. With a foaming wake the king's fleet of warriors stood out far from the land. When Kolga's sister [the billow] and the long keels dashed together, it was to the ear as if surf and cliffs were breaking against each other. Helgi bade them hoist the topsails higher. The fast-following seas kept tryst upon the hulls, whilst Eager's dreadful daughter strove to whelm the bows of the steer-steeds. But battle-bold Sigrun, from on high, saved them and their craft off Cliffholt. The king's brine-steed was wrested by main strength from Ran's hands, and that night the fair-found fleet rode safe once more in Unisvoe.

The foes gathered at Swarin's howe, mustering their host in angry mood. Quoth the god-born Godmund [Hodbrord's warder], 'Who is the king that steers these ships with a golden war-standard at his bows? No shield of peace, methinks, do I see in the van, but a halo of war wraps the Wickings about.'

Quoth Sinfiotli, hoisting a red shield, golden-rimmed, to the yard—he was a warder that could give a good answer, and bandy words with warriors—'Remember this evening, when thou art feeding the swine and leading the bitches to their swill, to make it known that the Wolfings from the East, in fighting mood, have come off Cliffholt. There in the midst of his fleet may Hodbrord find Helgi, that flight-spurning hero, who has often given the eagles their fill, whilst thou wast kissing the slave-girls at the querns.

Quoth Godmund: I would sate the ravens on thy carcase at Wolfstone before I would lead your bitches to their swill, or feed the hogs. The fiends bandy words with thee.

Quoth Sinfiotli: Thou, O Godmund, shalt sooner tend goats, and climb steep scaurs, holding a hazel club in thy hand. That is more to thy liking than the moot of the swords.

Quoth Godmund: Thou knowest little, my lord, of the stories of old, when thou bringest false charges against warriors. Thou thyself hast eaten wolves' meat and murdered thy brother. Thou hast often sucked wounds with cold mouth, and slunk, loathsome to all men, into the dens of wild beasts.

Quoth Sinfiotli: Thou, witch-hag that thou art, wast a sibyl in Warinsey, fashioning false prophecies. Thou didst say that thou wouldst have none of the mail-clad warriors to husband save Sinfiotli. Thou, hateful ogress, wast a Walkyrie, hideous, accursed of All-father. The Host of the chosen had well-nigh fought together for thy sake, thou false woman. On Saganess we two had a litter of nine wolves; I was the father of them all.

Quoth Godmund: Nay, thou wast no father of Wolves, that I can remember, since the ogre-maids gelt thee on Thorsness by Cliffholt. Thou wast Siggeir's step-son, and didst lie in the reindeer's lairs, out in the woods, used to the songs of the wolves. All manner of crimes fell to thy lot; thou didst rip up thine own brother's breast, and didst make thyself famous for abominations.

Quoth Sinfiotli: Thou wast Grani's dam on Braefield, golden-bitted thou rannest saddled for a race. I have ridden thee many a course, uphill and down dale, sitting in saddle on thy slim back, thou . . . .

Quoth Godmund: Thou wast a mannerless swain when thou wert milking Gollni's (the Giant's) goats; and now, for the second time, thou hagspawn, thou tatter-screen, wilt thou a longer tale?

Quoth Helgi: It would beseem you both far better, good Sinfiotli, to fight out your quarrel and gladden the eagle, than to bandy unprofitable words. Though the princes are my foes, yet a warrior should speak the truth, and brave, methinks, are Granmar's sons; they have proved on Moin's heath that they have the heart to wield their swords.

Now they rode their steeds Sweepwood and Swaywood with all speed to Sunham, through dewy dales and dusky glens; the sea of mist [air] shook as they passed by. They met the king in the gate of the court, and told him of the coming of his foes. Hodbrord was standing helm-hooded without the house, looking on the riding of his kinsmen: 'Why are the Hniflungs flushed with wrath?' [quoth he.]

Quoth Godmund: The lithe keels are turning their heads to our shore, ringed sea-stags, with long sail-yards, with many shields and smooth-planed oars, a great war-fleet, the gallant Wolfings. Fifteen battalions are landing, but out in Sogn are seven more thousand. At the dock by Cliffholt are lying surf-deer, swart-black, and fair with gold, there is by far the most of their host. Helgi will not put off the sword-moot.

Quoth Hodbrord: Bridle the fleet steeds to go forth and call a great levy! *Saddle* Spurwitni for Sparin's heath, Melni and Milni for Mirkwood. Let no man stay away that can bear a brand. Call up Hogni and the sons of Ring, Atli and Yngwi, Alf the old; they are all eager to waken war. Let the Wolsungs meet resistance.

With one swoop the yellow blades crossed at Wolf-Rock. Ever fought Helgi Hunding's slayer foremost in the foremost ranks, with stoutest mettle, spurning to fly. That hero's heart was steadfast. And now the Helmed Fairies, that watched over him, came down from heaven,—higher grew the clash of spears. Then spake Sigrun, winged war-fairy . . . . Hail, Prince of Yngwi's race, have joy of thy life, for thou hast felled the flight-spurning king that wrought the death of Eager. Thine, king, by right are now the red-rings and the mighty

64

maiden. Hail, king, and have joy of thy victory and thy realm!—Now the battle is ended . . . .

Sigrun to Hodbrord dying on the battle-field: Sigrun from Sevafell shall never, O King Hodbrord, rest in thy arms. Thy life and that of the sons of Granmar is at an end . . . .

Quoth Helgi: Thou canst not give good hap in all things, thou fairy, though some of this is the Fates' doing [not thine]. Bragi and Hogni fell this morning at Wolf-Rock, and at Styrcliff King Starkad, and Hrollaug's sons at Leaburgh: I was their slayer . . . . The fiercest king I ever saw, his trunk fought on when his head was off. Most of thy kinsmen lie corpses at Yordan. This slaughter was no work of thine, but thou wast fated to be the cause of feud among the Mighty.

II. *Day comes to Sigrun to tell her the news of her lover's death by his hand, saying:* Sorry am I, sister, to tell thee tidings of sorrow, and it is sore against my will to make my kinswoman weep. He fell this morning at Fetterholt that was the best of earthly princes, that trod upon the necks of kings.

Quoth Sigrun: May all the oaths that were sworn to Helgi, by the bright Lightning water and the ice-cold Rock of the Waves, sting thee now. May the ship that sails under thee sail not, even though thou have a fair wind aft! May the horse that runs under thee run not, yea, though thy foemen are following after thy life! May the sword that thou drawest bite not, save when it is whistling about thine own head! Helgi's death were but rightly avenged, if thou wert a wolf [outlaw] out in the woods, poor and joyless, and lacking meat save what thou couldst get from leaping on carrion corpses!

Quoth Day: Thou art mad and distraught, sister, to pray down curses on thine own brother. It was Woden alone that wrought all this evil, when he scattered runes of strife among kinsfolk. Thy brother offers thee red rings, all Wandilswe and Wardales, yea, the half of his land to recompense thy wrong to thee and thy sons, thou ring-dight lady.

Quoth Sigrun: Nevermore shall I sit happy at Sevafell, nor have joy of my life at morn or eventide; for nevermore shall I see the light flash on my lord's company, nor the war-steed with its gold bit bearing my king thither; nevermore shall I welcome the prince home. Helgi struck terror into his foemen and their kindred, so that they were like unto the fearful goats that run madly downhill from the wolf. Helgi was among other kings as it were a noble ash among the thorns, or as a young hart, flecked with dew, towering above the other deer, his antlers glittering against the very heaven. . . . . . .

III. *The dead Helgi enters the Halls of Woden with his company, and calls to King Hounding, his old enemy, to do service to him, saying:* Hounding, do thou make ready a foot-bath and kindle a fire for each of us, and tie up the hounds and bait the horses, and give the hogs their swill before thou goest to sleep! . . . . .

Sigrun said: Sigmund's son would have come by now, if he meant to come, from the halls of Woden. I have but faint hope of his coming, now that the eagles are sitting on the limbs of the ash and all the household are thronging to the Assembly of Dreams.

Sigrun's bondmaid sees Helgi and his company riding by in the dusk, and cries out: Is it a mere phantom that I think I see, or is the Doom of the Powers come?—Can dead men ride? Ye are pricking your steeds with the spur!—or have ye been granted leave to come home?

Helgi answered her: It is no mere phantom that thou thinkest thou seest, nor is it the end of the world, though we prick our steeds with the spur, but we have been granted leave to come home. Come out, O Sigrun from Sevafell, if thou desirest to see thy lord. The barrow is opened, Helgi is come, the sword-prints are gory on him. The king bids thee come to stay the bleeding of his wounds. It is time for me to ride along the reddening roads, to let my fallow steed tread the paths of air. I must be west of Windhelm's bridge [the sky bridge, i. e. rainbow] before Salgofni [chanticleer] awakens the mighty Host.

The bondmaid answered: Be not so mad as to go alone, thou sister of kings, to the houses of the Ghosts. All dead fiends of Hell wax stronger by night than in the bright daylight.

Sigrun goes out to meet her dead lord, and falls upon his neck and kisses him, saying: I am as glad to meet thee as are the greedy hawks of Woden when they scent the slain, their warm prey, or dew-spangled espy the brows of dawn. I will kiss thee, my dead king, ere thou cast off thy bloody mail-coat. Thy hair, my Helgi, is thick with rime, thy whole body is drenched with gory dew, thy hands are cold and dank. How shall I deliver thee from this, O my lord?

Helgi answered her: It is thine own doing, Sigrun from Sevafell, that Helgi is drenched with deadly dew. Thou weepest cruel tears, thou gold-dight, sun-bright lady of the South, before thou goest to sleep: every one of them falls bloody, dank cold, chilly, fraught with sobs, upon my breast. . . . Let us drink costly draughts, though we have lost both love and land! Let no man chant wailing dirges, though he see the wounds on my breast. Now are maidens, royal ladies, shut up in the barrow with us dead men!

Quoth Sigrun: I have made thee a bed here, Helgi, a very painless bed, thou son of the Wolfings. I shall sleep in thine arms, O king, as I should if thou wert yet alive.

Helgi answered: Now I swear that there shall never be a greater marvel, early or late, at Sevafell: for thou, the white daughter of Hogni, art sleeping in the arms of the dead; thou, a king's daughter, art come down alive into the barrow.

HELGI AND SWAVA

I. FRAGMENT.—*King Hiorward and Sigrlind. Hiorward sends Atli to woo Sigrlind to him; he is helped by a talking bird.*

The Bird says: HAST thou seen Sigrlind, Swafni's daughter, the fairest maid in this blissful world, though the lovely wives of King Hiorward in Glassgrove seem fair to men?—*Atli.* Thou wise bird, wilt thou talk more to Atli the son of Idmund?—*Bird.* I will, if the king will worship me, and I may choose what I will out of the king's house. —*Atli.* Thou shalt not choose Hiorward, nor his sons, nor any of his fair wives, nor one of the king's wives. Let us bargain together as friends do.—*Bird.* I will choose temples, and many high places, gold-horned kine from the king's stock, if I get Sigrlind to sleep in his arms, and follow the king of her own will.

Atli comes back to the King : We have had trouble and ill speed, our steeds foundered on the broad mountains; we had to wade across Sæmorn ; and then we were denied Swafni's daughter, the ring-endowed maid, whom we came to woo.

II. *The king wins her at last, and she bears him a son, and his father having been slain, he was silent and nameless. He goes one day out in the wood, and meets the Walkyria Swava, a king's daughter. She says—*

Helgi, my warrior, it will be long ere thou rulest over rings or the Sunfells—the eagle screamed early—if thou alway keep silence; though thou broodest over thy revenge.—*Helgi.* What gift wilt thou give with the name, thou bright-faced lady, since thou givest me these commands? Consider well thy words, I take no gift unless I am to have thyself to boot. *Then the Walkyria tells him where to find a magic sword, with which he is to win fame and avenge his father.*

I know where swords, two score and six, lie in Sigar's holm, but one is the best of them all, the curse of the war-net [mail], inwrought with gold. There is a ring in the hilt, a tang through the midst; an 'onn' in the point, for him that gets it; a blood-painted serpent lies along the edges, writhing his tail round the sword-knot.

O H., thou art not a well-advised king, although thou be a great champion ; thou madest the fire consume the halls of a king who had done no harm to thee. But thou lettest Rodmar rule over the treasures which our forefathers had. He (Rodmar) sits free from fear of foes, for he thinks he holds the heritage of an heirless race. (*K. Rodmar knew not that Helgi, Sigrlind's son, survived from the slaughter.*)

Helgi to his brother Hedin : Hail, Hedin ! what news hast thou to tell from Norway ? why art thou outlawed from thy country, and come alone to see us here ?—*Hedin.* Far greater is my guilt; I have chosen at the Bragi-toast thy king-born bride.—*Helgi.* Blame not thyself; the ale-talk of both of us may prove true. A king has challenged me to the field ; within three nights' time I must be there. I doubt if I shall ever come back; yet it may turn out well if I do not.—*Hedin.* Thou saidest that Rodmar had deserved goodwill and great gifts from thee, but it beseems thee better to redden thy sword than to give peace to thine enemies.

It was a witch, riding a wolf in the gloaming, that bade Hedin follow her. She knew that Sigrlind's son should be slain at Sigarsfield.

Helgi (*wounded to death*) sent Sigar [his friend] to fetch Eylimi's only daughter (Swava) : 'Tell her to make her ready quickly, if she would find her lord alive.'

Sigar goes to Swava and says : Helgi has sent me hither to speak to thee, Swava. He said he wished to see thee before he yielded up his breath.—*Swava.* How came hurt to Helgi Hiorwardson ? I sorely am stricken with grief—was it by sea or was it by sword, then I will

67

surely harm his slayer.—*Sigar*. This morning at Sigar's-field fell the best king under the sun. Alf has won, though it was in evil hour.

Swava comes to Helgi on the field of battle.

Helgi. Hail to thee, Swava! let not thy heart fail thee! this shall be our last meeting. My wounds are bleeding; the sword has cut right to my heart. I pray thee, Swava, if thou wilt hearken to my words—weep not, my lady!—to make ready the bed for Hedin, and lay thy love on him.—*Swava*. I had vowed in the home of my happiness, when thou, Helgi, didst endow me, that I would never, of my will, take any other to my arms after my lord's death.

Helgi dies, and Hedin bids farewell to Swava before going to revenge his brother.

Hedin. Kiss me, Swava! I will never come back to Strifeham, or Sunfell, before I have revenged the son of Hiorward, the best king under the sun!

HELGI AND KÁRA

When Helgi's father [Sevi?] was slain, he was saved by his foster-father Hagal, who sent him to be brought up in the hall of his enemy, giving him the name of his own son Hamal. When he was grown up Helgi left his foe's house, and bade a shepherd tell Heming whom he had fostered.

1. TELL Heming that Helgi knows who slew his father at B. (place, Bear-bay?); ye have cherished a wolf-cub among you, K. Harding, deeming that it was Hamal.

Blind the mischievous was sent to seek after him, and came to Hagal's house, where Helgi was hid in a bondmaid's dress, working the mill. When he saw him Blind said—

5. Hagal's bondmaid has fierce eyes, no slave-born maid is she that stands at the quern. The stones are cracking, the bin is shivering. Surely the prince is hardly entreated, when a lord such as he must grind the barley. The grip of the sword fits those hands better than the mill-handle.

12. *Hagal answered:* It is little wonder that the bin rattles as the king's bondmaid turns the handle. She was wont to ride above the clouds, and dared to fight as wickings use, before H. (*name uncertain*) made her captive. She is the sister of Sigar and Hogni. That is why the Wolfings' maid has such wild eyes.

After the battle, in which Helgi had slain Harding and avenged his father's death, Kara, the War-fairy, comes flying towards him.

19. *Kara said:* Who are ye that moor your ships by the shore? Where is your home, ye warriors? What are you awaiting at Bear-bay? Whither are you bound? *Helgi answers:* Hamal is letting his ships lie by off the shore. Our home is in Leesey. We are awaiting a fair wind at Bear-bay. We are bound for the east. *Kara says:* Where hast thou, King, wakened the war, and where didst thou sate the birds of the sister of Battle? Why is thy mailcoat flecked with blood? Why eat ye raw flesh, helmed as ye are? *Helgi answers:* The very last deed of the sons of the Wolfings west of the Main, if thou seekest to know, was

when I baited the bears in Bragholt and fed the eagle's brood full with my blade. Now, maiden, I have told thee why our meat is raw; we get little roast meat at sea, maiden! *Kara says:* Thou tellest of war; King Harding was made to bow low in the field before Helgi. The fight was joined, and Sevi was avenged, and the blood spirted on the edges of the brand. *Helgi says:* How canst thou tell, thou wise lady, that we be they that avenged Sevi? There are many keen wickings like unto us. *Kara says:* I was not far off, my lord, yestermorn when the chief was slain, though thou, son of Sevi, talkest covertly, and tellest of the war in strange riddles. I have seen thee before on the long ships, when thou stoodest at the bloody bows, and the ice-cold waves played about thee. Thou art striving to hide thee from me, my prince, but Halfdan's daughter knows thee well.

THE VOLSUNG STORY

The tale of the Volsungs and the related German Nibelung tradition are the most famous indigenous epics in the Germanic tradition. In modern times Richard Wagner, Friedrich Hebbel, and William Morris have used this material as the sources for literary masterpieces. It ranks with the Trojan story in its ability to capture the popular fancy.

Properly speaking the title "Volsunga Saga" should be applied only to the prose paraphrase, with expanded details, of the Eddic poems presented here. There are links to the Helgi tradition (supra) and to the saga of Ragnar Lodbrok, since Aslaug, Ragnar's bride, was the daughter of Sigurd and Brynhild. The Volsunga Saga was composed at quite a late date, probably the middle of the thirteenth century.

It is profitable to compare and contrast the Scandinavian story with the German Nibelungenlied. The latter was composed in the early thirteenth century by a South German poet. Although the content is of pagan origin, the tone and style are distinctly Christian and chivalric. Further, the poem is a formal, well organized, almost perfectly preserved masterpiece of one (unknown) author.

It is unfortunate that a Scandinavian Homer did not put together the Eddic poems in this cycle as a polished masterpiece comparable in formal organization to the Iliad or the Nibelungenlied. To fill in the details that are lacking in the poems the student is strongly urged to read a translation of the Volsunga Saga and William Morris' Sigurd the Volsung.

The Eddic poems are presented here in a sequence that corresponds to the saga and Morris' modern epic in four books of anapaestic couplets.

GRIPISSPÁ (THE PROPHECY OF GRIPIR)

Eylimi's son, Hjordis' brother, Gripir, was a noted seer and one of the wisest men of his time. Youthful and guileless Sigurd went to him to ask about his fate. Not too willingly Gripir reveals the tragic course of events that will take place in Sigurd's career.

FIRST SCENE.—*Sigurd at the gate of Gripi's castle.*
WHO dwells here in this hall? What is the name of this mighty king?—*Geiti, the warder, outside:* Gripi is the ruler's name, who reigns over the land and folk.—*Sigurd:* Is the good king at home in his land? Will the prince come and speak with me? A new comer wishes to talk with him; I would speedily see Gripi.—*Geiti:* The good king is sure to ask me this, Who is the man that asks speech of Gripi.—*Sigurd:* My name is Sigurd, Sigmund's son, but Hiordis was my mother.
SECOND SCENE. Now Geiti went in and told Gripi, ' Here is a man outside, a stranger; he is noble to look on, he would have speech of thee, my lord.'
The king of men goes out of the hall, and welcomes the strange hero, (saying): 'Take quarters here, Sigurd, would thou hadst come before ; but do thou, Geiti, see to Grani ! ' (*the horse.*) The two heroes, wise of counsel, began to speak and talk over many things, now that they had met.—*Sigurd:* Tell, if thou knowest, uncle dear, How will life turn out for Sigurd ?—*Gripi:* Thou shalt be the greatest man under the sun, and highest-born of all kings, free with thy gold, and chary of flight, noble to look on, and wise in speech.—*Sigurd:* Tell me, good king, more than I ask, if thou thinkest thou canst foresee it : What fortune shall first happen to me when I leave thy court ?—*Gripi:* Thou shalt first avenge thy father, and wreak all the wrong of Eylimi; thou shalt fell the brave and brisk sons of Hunding, thou shalt have victory.—*Sigurd:* Tell thy kinsman, noble king, very frankly, now that we have opened our hearts : Canst thou foresee exploits for me that shall soar very high under the borders of heaven ?—*Gripi:* Thou alone shalt slay the keen dragon, that lies in his greed at Giisten-heath ; thou shalt be the slayer of both Regin and Fafni; Gripi tells true.—*Sigurd:* Having wrought this slaughter by my valour, I shall have great treasure, as thou tellest me for truth ; consider in thy mind and tell me at length, How shall my life go then ?—*Gripi:* Thou shalt find Fafni's lair, and take up the fair treasure; load the gold on Grani's saddle, then thou shalt ride to Giuki's, victorious king.—*Sigurd:* Open thy heart, prophetic chief, and tell me more : When I am Giuki's guest, and leave him, how shall my life go then ?—*Gripi:* A king's daughter lies asleep on the mountain, bright in mail, wrapped in flames. Thou

71

shalt hew with thy keen sword, slitting the mail with the killer of Fafni.—*Sigurd:* The mail-coat is broken, the maid begins to speak, the lady is awakened out of her sleep: What then will she say to me that may be to my furtherance?—*Gripi:* She shall teach thee every mystery men wish to know, and to speak in every man's tongue, healing and leech-craft. Live and hail, my king!—*Sigurd:* Now that is done, and I have learnt the wisdom, and am ready to ride abroad, consider in thy mind, and tell me at length, How then shall my life go? —*Gripi:* Thou shalt light on Heimi's dwelling, and be the glad guest of the great king. I have told all, Sigurd, that I can foresee; ask no further of Gripi.—*Sigurd:* What thou now sayest makes me sorry, because thou canst see further, O king; thou canst see a great sorrow for Sigurd, that is why thou wilt not, Gripi, tell it me clearly.— *Gripi:* I neglected whilst young 'the craft of prophecy.' I am not rightly called prophet, nor a true seer; what I knew is gone.—*Sigurd:* I know no man above ground that can see farther forward than thou; hide it not, though it be foul, or though there be some blot in my life.—*Gripi:* There are no blots in thy life, hold that in mind; for thy name shall ever be high while men live, my hero.—*Sigurd:* That is least to my mind to part from thee thus. Shew me my path, for all is predestined, if thou wilt, my uncle.—*Gripi:* Now I will tell thee, Sigurd, clearly, as thou forcest me so to do; thou shalt surely know that I lie not: a day is set for thy death.—*Sigurd:* I would not have thine anger on me, O king, but rather get thy good counsel. Now I must know for sure, though it be not pleasant, what lies before my hand.—*Gripi:* There is a maid at Heimi's, fair to see, they call her Brunhild, Budli's daughter, a proud lady, but Heimi, that great king, fosters the proud maid.—*Sigurd:* What is that to me, though there be a maid, fair to see, fostered at Heimi's? Thou shalt tell me this exactly, Gripi, because thou seest all fate before thee.—*Gripi:* This Heimi's foster-daughter, fair to see, shall rob thee of all thy happiness; thou shall not sleep a slumber, nor go to court, nor care for any man, except thou look on that maid.—*Sigurd:* What comfort is there set for Sigurd? Tell me this, Gripi, if thou knowest it: shall I buy the maid with dowry, that fair king's daughter?—*Gripi:* Ye shall swear all oaths fully, but ye shall hold few. When thou hast been Giuki's guest one night, thou shalt remember no more the brave foster-daughter of Heimi.— *Sigurd:* How is that, Gripi, tell it me; seest thou any lack of honour in my mind, that I should break my word to the maiden whom I loved with all my heart?—*Gripi:* Thou shalt be the victim of another's treason, and shalt suffer for Grimhild's schemes. That bright-haired lady shall offer thee her daughter, drawing her wiles around thee.— *Sigurd:* Shall I then marry into Gunnar's family and wed Gudrun? That would be a good match if no heart-sores befall me.—*Gripi:* Grimhild will surely beguile thee, she will stir thee up to woo Brynhild for Gunnar the king of the Goths, and thou shalt straightway promise her to go.—*Sigurd:* There is ill luck then before my hands, I see so much; my life goes clean wrong, if I am to woo the noble maid, that I love best, for another.—*Gripi:* Ye shall all of you, Gunnar and Hogni, and thou the third, swear oaths to each other. Ye shall take each other's form, Gunnar and thou, when ye are on the way. I lie not.—*Sigurd:* How can that be? how can we change face and form when we are on the way? Some other treason must surely be brewing. Say on, Gripi.—*Gripi:* Thou hast put on Gunnar's face and form, but thy speech and thine heart are still thine own. Thou shalt betroth thee Heimi's haughty foster-daughter. . . . . . .—*Sigurd:* I think that is the worst, that, [if this be so,] I shall be called faithless among men. I would never treacherously ensnare the king's daughter whom I honour most.—*Gripi:* Thou shalt sleep, prince, by the maid as if she were thy mother. Therefore thy name, O king, shall be held high while men live.—*Sigurd:* Shall the famous Gunnar wed the noble lady, —tell me, Gripi,—after she has slept those nights by my side? It is not to be looked for.—*Gripi:* Both bridals shall be drunk together, thine and Gunnar's, in Giuki's hall; when ye come home ye shall change forms again, but each shall keep his own heart.—*Sigurd:* What after happiness will there be in this match? tell me, will it turn out to Gunnar's happiness or my own?—*Gripi:* No, thou shalt remember the oaths, though thou must be silent; thou wilt not begrudge Gudrun her luck; but Brynhild will think she is ill-matched, and she will contrive means for revenge.—*Sigurd:* What redress shall she get, since we beguiled her? she having my sworn words, none fulfilled, and no happiness.— *Gripi:* She will persuade Gunnar that thou hast not kept thy oaths to him, when he, the son of Giuki, trusted thee with all his heart.—*Sigurd:* What is this? Gripi, tell it me, shall I be guilty of this charge, or does the belauded lady belie me and herself? Tell me this, Gripi.—*Gripi:* The mighty maid shall, for wrath and out of her despair, deal ill with thee. It was no fault of thine, though ye did ensnare that fair princess. —*Sigurd:* Shall the brave Gunnar, and Gothorm, and Hogni follow her egging afterward? Shall the sons of Giuki redden the edge of the spear with my blood, their kinsman? Tell me more, Gripi.—*Gripi:* Gudrun's heart shall be cruelly used when her brothers slay thee. That wise lady shall nevermore be happy; this is Grimhild's fault. I will comfort thee with this, my prince, that this blessing shall rest on thy life that no better man shall ever come upon earth under the seat of the sun, than thou, Sigurd, shall be held.

Sigurd: Let us part in peace. No man can withstand his fate. And thou, Gripi, hast done just as I bade thee. Thou wouldst fain have told my life brighter, if thou hadst been able.

REGINSMÁL (WORDS OF REGIN)
FÁFNISMÁL (WORDS OF FÁFNIR)
SIGRDRIFOMÁL (WORDS OF SIGRDRIFA)

Regin, son of Reidmar and brother of Fáfnir and Otter, was Sigurd's foster father. He was a dwarf and, like many others of his race, a skilled craftsman, but also wise and ruthless. Regin told Sigurd about the events at Andvari's Falls, where a dwarf named Andvari lived in the form of a pike. Odin, Hoenir, and Loki came to the cataract and saw Otter, in the shape of a true otter, feasting on a salmon. Loki killed the beast with a stone, and the gods flayed it. That evening Reidmar was their host, and when he saw the otter's skin, he demanded wergild consisting of as much gold as might be needed to cover the pelt. Loki had to find the precious metal, and he caught Andvari, in the shape of a pike, in a net. He extracted a great hoard from Andvari, even to a small gold ring, on which the dwarf put a curse. The otter's pelt was covered save for one whisker; and when Reidmar demanded that it be covered, Loki had to surrender the ring. In so doing, he reiterated the terrible curse of Andvari that no one would ever have any but ill luck from owning his hoard.

Fáfnir killed his father and took the hoard for himself. Transforming himself into a fearful dragon, he brooded over the hoard on Gnita Heath. Regin egged Sigurd on to slay Fáfnir, for which purpose he forged a marvelous sword, Gram, from two pieces of the broken sword of Sigurd's father, Sigmund. Sigurd mounted the great horse Grani, out of the line of Odin's fabulous eight-legged Sleipnir, and slew Fáfnir, who, dying, once more repeated the curse.

Regin demanded as wergild for his brother only the heart of the dragon. Sigurd put the organ on a spit and touched it as it roasted. He tasted the blood and was able to understand the language of birds (cf. Melampus, Balaam, and Elwood P. Dowd in Harvey). Three pies were discussing the affair and warned that Sigurd should slay Regin, who planned to double-cross Sigurd and keep the entire treasure. Sigurd followed this advice and then seized the hoard.

After his heroic deeds, Sigurd awakened the Valkyrie Sigrdrifa and received her sage advice in the form of the maxims similar to those in the Hávamál. Vigfusson and Powell have put together the three poems which contain this material as "The Old Play of the Volsungs".

I. LOKI *and* ANDWARI.—*Loki.* WHAT is that fish that swims in the stream, and does not know how to keep out of danger? Ransom thou thy head from death, give up thy hoard.—*Andwari.* My name is Wideawake, Oin was my father, many a fall have I swum up. An evil Norn doomed me long ago to swim in water.

Loki. Tell me, Andwari, if thou wilt keep thy life on earth, what penance awaits the sons of men who revile one another?—*Andwari.* Heavy is their penance : They must wade through Whelm-ford. False words against another strike deep roots of retribution.

II. LOKI *and* RODMAR.—*Loki.* Here is the gold for thee, verily thou hast a great ransom for my head. Luck shall not fall to thy son ; it shall be the death of you both.—*Rodm.* Thou gavest gifts indeed, and no gifts of love, thou gavest not with whole heart. It should cost you your lives if I knew this disaster was to come.—*Loki.* There is a worse still in store, as I know, a deadly feud among thy offspring. They who shall be under this curse are still unborn.—*Rodm.* I shall enjoy the red gold as long as I live; I fear nought thy threats. Get ye home.

III. RODMAR *and* LYNGHEID.— *Rodmar (deadly wounded, to his daughters).* Lyngheid and Lofnheid! Behold, I am dying! Manifold are the woes of men.— *Lyngheid.* How can sisters revenge their father's death on their own brother !

IV. LYNGHEID *to* REGIN *(her brother).* Call gently on thy brother for inheritance and redress, for it ill beseems thee, at sword's point to call on Fafni for treasures.

V. HNIKAR [*Woden*] *and* SIGFRED.—Tell me, Nikar, as thou knowest the omens of gods and men, what is the best omen in battle whilst the swords are sweeping.

Nikar. Many good omens there are, if men but knew them, while the swords are sweeping. It is a good omen for a warrior to be followed by the dark raven. It is another, if thou be without thy house ready for thy journey and thou see two proud warriors standing in the path. It is a third, if thou hear a wolf howling underneath the branches of an ash, then if thou see them going before thee, thou wilt gain victory over thy antagonists. It is a most fatal omen if thou stumble on thy feet when marching to battle for Evil Fairies stand on either side of thee, wishing to see thee wounded. Combed and washed shall every man be, and take his morning meal: for no one knows where he may lodge at night. Ill it is to outrun one's luck.

VI. FAFNI *and* SIGFRED.—*Fafni (mortally wounded).* Boy, O boy! whose son art thou, and what man's child art thou that thou hast reddened thy keen brand on Fafni? the sword has struck me to the heart. —*Sigfred (the unborn, wants to hide his name).* My name is Noble deer; I came into the world a motherless child; I had no father like the sons of men. I stand alone.—*Fafni.* Tell me if thou hadst no father like the sons of men, by what marvel wert thou born? *(here something is lost)* . . . —*Sigfred.* My race is unknown to thee, I think, and myself also.— *Fafni.* Who egged thee on? why wert thou persuaded to seek my life? Thou keen-eyed boy, thou hadst a bitter father. To the unborn . . . —*Sigfred.* My heart egged me on; my hands helped me, and this my sharp sword. An old man is seldom valiant, if he was cowardly in his

75

youth.—*Fafni*. Behold! if thou grow up for the face of thy friends, one would see thee fight in wrath; but now thou art in bonds and captive. A prisoner's heart is ever throbbing.—*Sigfred*. Why blamest thou me, because I am far from my father's care? I am no bondman, though I be captive; thou hast felt that my hands were free.—*Fafni*. Thou talkest none but words of hate, though I tell thee but the truth. The ringing gold, and the fire-red hoard; these rings shall be thy death!— *Sigfred*. Every one longs to enjoy his riches to his last day; because every one must needs sometime go hence to Hell.—*Fafni*. The doom of the Norns [death] will overtake thee off the (*nearest*) headlands ... Thou shalt drown in the water if thou rowest in a gale. The doomed man's death lies everywhere.

WISDOMS.—*Sigfred*. Tell me, Fafni, since they call thee wise and of great knowledge—Who are the Norns, the midwives of mankind, who chose the child from the mother's womb?—*Fafni*. The Norns are of most sundry races, they have no common kin; some are of Anse-race, some of Elve-race, some Dwale's (Dwarf's) daughters.

Sigfred. Tell me, Fafni, etc.: What is that holm called, where Swart and the Anses shall mingle blood together?—*Fafni*. Unshapen is the name of the reef, where all the gods shall hold a lance play. Bilrost [Rainbow] shall break as they pass over the bridge, and swim their steeds through the waters.

Fafni. I carried the helm of terror over the sons of men, when I lay on the Hoard. I thought myself stronger than all beside, finding none my peer.—*Sigfred*. The helm of terror is of little help in deadly fray. A man soon finds, when he comes among others, that no one is peerless. —*Fafni*. I spouted venom when I lay on the great hoards of my father. ... —*Sigfred*. Thou fierce Dragon, thou madest a great blast, and a hard heart. All the greater the hate will be among the sons of men, if they have that helm.—*Fafni*. I counsel thee, Sigfred, do thou take my counsel; ride straight home. The ringing gold, and the fire-red hoard; these rings shall be thy death!—*Sigfred*. I have heard thy counsel, yet I shall ride towards the gold that lies on the heath. But thou, Fafni, lie there in thy death throes till Hell take thee!—*Fafni*. (Beware) Regin betrayed me; so he will thee; he will be the death of us both. Now, Fafni, I shall yield my life. Thy strength hath prevailed. (*Fafni dies, Regin comes in.*)

VII. REGIN *and* SIGFRED.—*Regin*. Hail, Sigfred! thou hast won the victory, and slain Fafni. Of all men who tread the earth, verily thou art the bravest born.—*Sigfred*. It cannot be known, when the Sons of the Blessed Gods meet all together, who is the bravest born. There is many a bold man who has never reddened his sword in another's breast.—*Regin*. Thou art glad, Sigfred, and rejoicest in thy victory, now thou wipest Gram [thy sword] in the grass. Thou hast given my brother his death-wound; though I myself took share therein.— *Sigfred*. It was thou who madest me to ride hither over the holy hills; the fierce Dragon would still be enjoying his life and hoard, hadst thou not challenged my courage.—*Regin*. Sit down, Sigfred, and roast Fafni's heart at the fire whilst I go to sleep. I will take a morsel of the heart after this draught of blood.—*Sigfred*. Thou stoodest aloof, when

I reddened my sharp sword on Fafni. I matched my strength against the Dragon's might, whilst thou wast hiding in the heath.—*Regin.* Long indeed might the Dragon, that old Giant, have lain on the heath, if thou hadst not the help of the sword that I made thee, this sharp brand of mine.—*Sigfred.* Courage is better than a good brand, when the wroth meet in fray, for I have seen a brave man win the day with a blunt sword. The brave fares better than the coward in the game of war; the cheery man fares better than the whiner, whatever betide him.

VIII. *The* THREE TALKING PIES *and* SIGFRED (*Sigfred is sitting beside the sleeping Regin, roasting the dead Fafni's heart at the fire. The birds speak from the tree above him*).

First Pie. Let him send the hoary Counsellor quick to Hell, shorter by the head, then all the gold shall be his, all the hoard that Fafni lay on.

Second Pie. He is right foolish if he spare any longer his dangerous foe. Lo! where Regin lies, who has plotted his death. He [Sigfred] cannot guard against it.

Third Pie. Let him shorten the rime-cold Giant by the head, and enter into his hoard; then he will be sole owner of all the riches Fafni had.

Sigfred (*who, having tasted the heart, understands the birds' talk*). The Fates shall not fall so ill, that Regin shall sentence me to death; for both the brothers shall quickly go hence to Hell.

IX. SIGRDRIFA *and* SIGFRED.—*Sigrd.* (*awakening from the enchanted sleep*). Long have I slept, long have I slumbered; the spells bind men long. Woden wrought this, that I could not break from the rods of sleep. Hail Day! hail Day's sons! Hail Night and her sister [Earth]! Look with gracious eyes upon us, and bless us both as we sit here. Hail Anses! hail Goddesses! and hail mother Earth! Give to us, two goodly lovers, counsels and wisdom; and healing hands as long as we live!

THE CHARMS OF SIGRDRIFA, *which she spake to Sigfred.*—**Runes of Victory** thou must know, if thou wilt have victory; and *thou shalt* grave them on thy sword-hilt; some on the rims, some on the carnage-brands, and twice name **Ty.**

Runes of Love thou must know, if thou wilt not have another's wife in whom thou trustest betray thy trust. Cut them on the horn, and on the back of the hand, and mark **Need** on thy nail.

[**Runes of Ale** thou must know . . .] Cross thy cup against ill; and throw leak into the liquor, [then I know that thy mead will never be poisoned.]

Runes of Help thou must know, if thou wilt help to deliver a woman of a child. Grave them on the palm of the hand, and clasp it on the wrist. and cry upon the Fairies for help.

Runes of Sea shalt thou grave, if thou wilt save the sailsteeds afloat. Grave them on the bow and on the rudder-blade, and mark **Eld** [Rune] on thy oar. Be the wave ever so steep, or the billows never so black, thou shalt come safe from the deep.

Runes of Branches thou must know, if thou wilt be a leech, and learn to search a wound. Thou shalt grave them on the bark, and on the stock of a tree whose branches lean eastwards.

Runes of Speech thou must know, if thou wilt that no one may harm thee in a feud. Wind them; weave them; put them all together at the husting when the assembly is going into full court.

Runes of Mind thou shalt know if thou wilt be wiser than all other men.

*　　*　　*　　*　　*　　*　　*　　*

Sigrdrifa. Now, my hero, as thou hast the choice, choose either silence or speech. All evils are meted out [predestined].—*Sigfred.* I will not flinch, yea, though I know I am a doomed man, I was not born a coward; I will cherish all thy loving counsels as long as I live.

Sigrdrifa's Counsels.—*Sigrdrifa.* I counsel thee *firstly*: Avoid thou offence towards thy kinsmen; even if they harm thee, revenge it not. It will do thee good when thou art dead.

I counsel thee *secondly*: Swear no oath, except it be true. Perjury strikes fearful roots. Most wretched is the truce-breaker.

I counsel thee *thirdly*: Do not plead in court against an ignorant man: for a fool may drop worse words than he knows of. Thou hast no choice: if thou holdest thy peace thou art either held a coward, or his words are held to be true.—The home verdict is a parlous matter, unless it be good;—slay him the next day, and thus requite people for their lie.

I counsel thee *fourthly*: If a witch full of evil be in thy way, better go on than sleep there, though the night overtake thee. The sons of men need an eye of foresight, wherever the fray rages, for balewise women (evil Fairies) often stand near the way, blunting swords and mind.

I counsel thee *fifthly*: Though thou seest fair brides on the bench, let them not hinder thy sleep. Do not allure women to kisses.

I counsel thee *sixthly*: Though there be high words bandied at the banquet, never quarrel with drunken men: wine is a great wit-stealer. Revellings and ale have often brought men grief of heart, death to some, to some curses. Manifold are the evils of men.

I counsel thee *seventhly*: If thou hast to fight out a quarrel with dauntless men, better to fight than be burnt in the house.

I counsel thee *eighthly*: Beware of evil, and avoid staves of falsehood. Betray no maid nor man's wife, nor lead them to shame.

I counsel thee *ninthly*: Care thou for corses, wherever on earth thou findest them, be they sick-dead, or sea-dead, or weapon-dead. Make a bath for the departed man; wash his hands and head; comb him and dry him, ere he be put in coffin; and bid him sleep sweetly.

I counsel thee *tenthly*: Trust thou never the oath of an outlaw's son, if thou hast slain his brother, or felled his father. There is a wolf in a young son, though he be comforted with gold. Feuds and hates are not sleepy, nor malice either. The warrior, who is to be the chief among men, must needs have the choicest wits and weapons.

I counsel thee *eleventhly*: Beware of evil in all thy ways. For thee I can forecast no long life. Mighty feuds have arisen [which will cause thy death].

78

BROT AF SIGURDARKVIDA (FRAGMENT OF A SIGURD LAY)

The first half of this noble poem and possibly part of the end are missing in the principal manuscript of the Poetic Edda, the Codex Regius. There are some variants from other traditions (e.g., the raven and the eagle) in this highly dramatic fragment, and there is no pyre scene (possibly in a missing finale). However corrupt the existing text may be, we do have here what surely must have been one of the most impressive of all the poems in the collection.

The end of a song describing how, by treason, Sigurd was slain by Gothorm in a wood.

[*Hogni quoth :* . . . ' What is Sigurd's] guilt, that thou wouldst take the hero's life ?'—*Quoth Gunnar :* ' Sigurd swore oaths to me, swore oaths, that are all belied ; he beguiled me when he should have been a true keeper of all oaths.'—*Quoth Hogni :* ' It is Brynhild that has egged your hate to do this wickedness, to bring about this crime. She grudges Gudrun her good match, and grudges thy possession of herself.'

Some gave Gothorm boiled wolf's flesh, some sliced serpents, some . . . . before they could persuade him to lay hands on the gentle hero.

Sigurd died south of the Rhine. A raven called loudly from the tree [to the murderers]: 'Atli will redden the sword upon you, he shall overcome you . . . . for your broken oaths.'

He listened much ; he caught up many words. The warrior bethought him of what the twain, the raven and the eagle on the tree, were talking when they were on their way home.

Gudrun, Giuki's daughter, stood without, and this was the first word she spoke: ' Where is Sigurd, the king of men, that my brothers are riding in the van ?'—Hogni made answer to her words: ' We have hewn Sigurd asunder with the sword, the grey horse may droop his head for ever over the dead king.'

Then spake Brunhild, Budli's daughter: ' Have great joy of your weapons and hands. Sigurd would have ruled everything as he chose, if he had kept his life a little longer. It was not meet that he should so rule over the host of the Goths, and the heritage of Giuki, who begot five sons that delighted in war and the havoc of battle.'

Brunhild laughed, the whole house rang: ' Have long joy of your hands and weapons, since ye have slain the keen king.' Then spake Gudrun, Giuki's daughter: ' Thou speakest very marvellously . . . . murderous mood shall be revenged.'

Then spake Brunhild, Budli's daughter: ' Egg me or stay me—the deed is done.' . . . . They were all silent at that word, no one could understand how she could weep when she spoke of what she had laughed at when she egged them on. . . . .

The evening was far gone, they had drunk deep, they had talked their fill. . . . . They all slept when they came into their beds, Gunnar alone of them all kept waking longer. . . . .

Brunhild, Budli's daughter, kinswoman of kings, awakened a little before the day, *saying*, ' I dreamed evil dreams in my sleep, Gunnar, it was all chilly in the hall, I had a cold bed, but thou, O king, didst ride, bereft of joy, fettered on thy feet, into the ranks of thy foes. So shall all the race of you Hniflungs be reft of strength, for ye are oath-breakers. Rememberest thou that clearly, Gunnar? how ye twain [Sigurd and thyself] did let your blood run together in the footprint [swearing brotherhood], but now thou hast repaid him with ill for it all, for showing himself ever the first of men. It was proved when he rode in his boldness to woo me, how the host-queller kept his oaths to the young king [yourself]. The good king laid the gold inlaid wound-wand between us, its edges outside were wrought in the fire, but the inner part [of the blade] was stained with drops of venom. . . . .

GUDRÚNARKVIDA (THE LAY OF GUDRUN)

Here is what amounts to a lamentation, moving and gentle in tone. The silent weeping of this noble heroine is in sharp contrast to the boisterous protests of Brynhild against her fate, accentuated by screaming geese and rattling tableware. For this reason some scholars have identified in it a trend to the psychoanalysis more kin to the literature of the twentieth century than to that of the eleventh. The almost complete lack of action also sets this poem apart from the others in the collection.

IT was in the olden time, Gudrun was nigh to death, as she sat sorrowful over Sigurd. She made no loud cry, nor wrung her hands, nor wept as other women use. The wise men came and tried to soothe her heavy heart.

Nevertheless Gudrun could not weep, she was so oppressed, her heart was like to break.

The gentle ladies, dight with gold, sate before her. Each of them told her her own sorrows, the bitterest woes she had endured. Then spake Giaflaug, Giuki's sister: 'I hold myself the most forlorn woman on earth. I have lost five husbands, two daughters, five sisters, eight brothers. I alone am left alive.'

Nevertheless Gudrun could not weep, she was so oppressed at her husband's death, so heavy-hearted over the king's corpse.

Then spake Herborg, the queen of Hunland: 'I have heavier losses to tell. My seven sons from the land of the South, and my husband the eighth, fell in battle. My father and mother, my four brothers, the wind of the deep played over them, the billow dashed them against the gunwales. They had none but me to wash them, none but myself to bury them, none but myself to lay out their corpses. All this I suffered in one season, nor was there any one to comfort me. After this I was taken captive, and for seven years held a prisoner of war [as the vilest of women], and put in bondage. I had to dress and bind the shoes on the lord's wife every morning. She would threaten me in her jealousy, and drove me with heavy stripes. I never saw a better goodman anywhere, nor ever anywhere a worse goodwife.'

Nevertheless Gudrun could not weep, she was so oppressed at her son's death, and so heavy-hearted over the king's [her husband's] corpse.

Then spake Goldrand, Giuki's daughter: 'Thou knowest not, foster-mother, though thou be wise, how to comfort the young wife.' She bade them uncover the king's body, and swept the sheet from off Sigurd, casting it to the ground before his wife's knees. 'Look on thy love, lay thy mouth to his lips as if thou wert clasping thy living lord.'

Gudrun cast one look upon him, she saw the king's hair dripping with blood, his keen eyes dead, his breast scored by the sword. Then she fell upon the pillow, with loosened hair and reddened cheek; her tears trickled like rain-drops down to her knee. And now Gudrun, Giuki's daughter, wept so, that the tears soaked through her tresses.

Then spake Goldrand, Giuki's daughter: 'The love of you two is the greatest I ever saw upon earth. Thou couldst never rest, my sister, within doors or out, save thou wert at Sigurd's side.'

Then spake Gudrun, Giuki's daughter: 'As the tall garlick above the grasses, or like a high-legged hart among the fleet deer, or like ember-red gold to the gray silver, or like the glittering gem upon a thread of beads, so was my Sigurd among the sons of Giuki, above all lords beside. Among the king's champions I was held higher than any other maid of Woden, but now I am brought as low as a willow shrunk of her leaves, by the death of the king; at board and at bed I miss my gossip. It was the sons of Giuki, it was the sons of Giuki that caused my misery, the sore tears of their sister. May ye [keep land and lieges] according as ye kept your sworn oath. Thou shalt never profit by the gold, Gunnar, those rings shall be thy death, for the oath's sake which thou didst swear to Sigurd. There was far greater joy in the court when my Sigurd saddled Grani, and ye two went forth to woo Brunhild, that accursed being, in an evil day.'

Then spake Brunhild, Budli's daughter: 'May that being lack both husband and children that moved thee to tears, Gudrun, and gave thee the power of speech this day!'

Then spake Goldrand, Giuki's daughter: 'Hold thy peace, thou hateful woman, from such words. Thou hast been an Evil Fate to princes, ... a sore sorrow to seven kings, and a bereaver of many a wife.'

Then spake Brunhild, Budli's daughter: 'Atli, my brother, the son of Budli, alone wrought this woe, when, in the hall of the people of the Huns, we saw the fire of the lair [Sigurd's spoils, Fafni's hoard]. For that journey of Sigurd I have paid dearly, [for that never-to-be-forgotten sight].'

She stood by the pillar, she . . . . Fire was kindled in the eyes of Brunhild, Budli's daughter, the venom spirted from her mouth when she saw the wounds of Sigurd.

SIGURDARKVIDA IN SKAMMA (THE SHORT LAY OF SIGURD)

Here is the same story as the previous one, but told from Brynhild's standpoint.

IT was in the days of old that Sigurd, the young Wolsung who had slain [Fafni], came to Giuki's. He received the troth-plight with two brothers; the doughty heroes interchanged oaths. They [the sons of Giuki] offered him the maid Gudrun, Giuki's daughter, and a great dowry; they drank and took counsel together many a day, the young Sigurd and the sons of Giuki, till they went to woo Brynhild with Sigurd riding in their company, the young Wolsung, ... he was to win her if he could get her. . . . The Southern hero laid a naked sword, his sign-painted brand, between them twain; nor did the Hunnish king ever kiss her, neither take her into his arms; he handed the young maiden over to Giuki's son.

She knew no guilt in her life, nor was any evil found in her when she died, no blame in deed or in thought, it was the cruel Fates that meddled. She sat out of doors alone in the evening, she spake once and no more:—I will have Sigurd, that young man, in my arms, or else die. I have spoken a word that I repent of now. Gudrun is his wife, and I am Gunnar's. The foul Fates have doomed us long sorrow.

She would often walk about the house 'full of anger,' with her heart sore every night when Gudrun and her husband went to bed, and Sigurd the Hunnish king clasped her, his fair wife, in the linen. 'I walk loveless, husbandless, sonless; I must lull myself with cruel thoughts.' Out of this passion she whetted herself to murder. 'Thou shalt straightway lose my land and myself, Gunnar, I will live no more with thee; I will go back where I dwelt before with my next-of-kin; there I will sit and dream my life out, unless thou wilt put Sigurd to death and make thyself king above all others. Let the son perish with the father; "One cannot foster a wolf-cub long." Revenge is sought by every son, and "The feud is fresh as long as a son lives."'

Gunnar was sad and bent down his head; he sat all day casting about in his mind, for he did not know clearly what was most seemly for him to do, or what was best for him to do, for he knew that he was [beholden] to the Wolsung, and that he would have a great loss in [losing] Sigurd. He cast about as long on this side as on that. It was not every day's hap for a queen to leave her king. 'Brunhild, the child of Budli, is better than all; she is a paragon among women. I would sooner lose my life than lose that maiden's dowry.' He betook him to call Hogni to counsel with him, for he ever put most trust in him. 'Now wilt thou betray the King [Sigurd] for his wealth? It were sweet to own the hoard of the Rhine, and wield that wealth in happiness, and sit and enjoy it in peace.' With that Hogni made answer, 'Surely it beseems us not to do such a deed . . . . the strong ties of marriage, the sworn oaths, the oaths sworn, and the plighted faith. We know no men on earth happier than we, while we four rule the people, and this Hunnish champion is alive, nor any mightier kindred on earth, if we five were to beget young sons, and could keep up and multiply our goodly race. I know well whence this . . . . proceeds; great are the wiles of Brunhild.' —*Gunnar answers:* ' Let us make Gothorm do the murder, our younger simpler brother; he was outside all the sworn oaths, the oaths sworn, the plighted faith.'

It was easy to egg the reckless youth; the sword pierced Sigurd to the heart.

The hero took his revenge there in the hall; the bright sword Gram flew out of his hand and struck Gothorm. His enemy fell in two pieces, the head and arms falling one way, and the legs and belly falling down where he stood.

Gudrun was sleeping peacefully in the bed, but she awoke to woe. She was bathed in the blood of Frey's friend [Sigurd]. She wrung her hands so sorely that the strong-hearted hero rose up in the bed. 'Weep not so terribly, Gudrun, thou fair young bride, for thy son is alive. Yea, I have yet a young heir, though he will hardly escape from this house of foes. They have dealt sorely and foolish by themselves, though they have cunningly contrived these counsels. They will never ride to the assembly with such a brother-in-law [though they be all together]. I know very well how things are: Brunhild alone wrought all this wickedness; she loved me above all other men, but I never dealt wrongfully by Gunnar. I observed our kinship by marriage, and the oaths we swore, lest I should be called the lover of his wife.'

The lady breathed a sigh, but the king breathed out his life: so loud was the cry of Giuki's daughter that the cups rang on the wall, and the geese screamed in the yard.

Then Brunhild, Budli's daughter, laughed once and no more, with all her heart, when she heard it in the bed, the loud cry of Giuki's daughter.

Then spake Gunnar, the king of men: 'Thou laughest not for joy now, thou revengeful woman, or for any good. . . . Why dost thou put away the white colour of thy face, thou mother of evils? I hold thee death-doomed. Thou wert most deserving of this, that we should smite down Atli before thine eyes, that thou shouldst see bleeding wounds on thy brother, and shouldst have to bind his gory wounds.'

Brunhild answered: 'No man can deny it thee, Gunnar, thou hast fulfilled a deed. Atli cares little for [thy pride], his breath will outlast thine, and he will ever be of greater might. I will tell thee, Gunnar, thou knowest it very well thyself, how ye first began the fray. I was young [and not full-grown], and richly nurtured in my brother's house, and I desired not that any husband should wed me, till ye Giukings, three mighty kings, rode into the court on horseback; but would they had never ridden thither. Moreover, Atli spake secretly with me, saying that he would never give me my portion save I agreed to be given in marriage, neither gold nor land, nor any part of my rightful wealth,

84

which was given to me when I was yet a babe, and the ounces which were counted out to me while I was yet a babe. Then my mind was turning this way and that over the matter, whether I should betake me, boldly clothed in mail, to fighting and felling corses, because of my brother, or no. It would become known to all people as a defiance to my kinsmen, but in the end we joined covenants together. I inclined rather to take the dowry, the red rings of Sigmund's son, but I would take no other man's ounces. . . . To love him only, not choosing first this, then that, my mind was not turning this way and that. 1 promised myself to the mighty king as he sat with the gold on Grani's saddle. He was not like you in the eyes, nor in any part of his countenance, though ye think yourselves great kings. . . . . . Atli shall find this out afterward, when he hears of my violent death [at my own hands], that I will not, like a weak-minded woman, set my love on another woman's husband.' . . . . . .

Up rose Gunnar, king of men, and threw his arms about his wife's neck; one by one they all came up, with kindly hearts, to try and stay her, but she cast her husband from her neck, nor would she let any one stay her from her long journey [to Hell]. Then he called Hogni to take counsel with him. 'I would that all men should come into the hall, thy men and mine together, for we are in great need, to see if they may stay her from slaying herself. . . . .' Hogni made answer once and no more. ' Let no man stay her from the long journey, that she may never be born again; she was a curse even from her mother's knees, she has been born ever to evil, a grief to the heart of many a man.'

She turned [*scornfully*] from their talk, where she was dealing out her treasures; she [was looking over all her wealth] . . . . bondmaids, and house-women. She put on a [golden mail-coat], in no happy mood, before she thrust herself through with the edge of the sword.

She sank on the bolster on one side, and began to . . . . wounded as she was with the brand. ' Come hither, all ye of my bondmaids that wish for gold, and take it at my hands. I will give each of you a broidered gown, a plaid, and dyed linen, bright raiment.'

They held their peace, ... made answer all together, ' . . . . to do honour.' Till the young linen-veiled lady spake again wisely, ' I will have no man . . . . lose his life for our sake . . . .' the costly flour of Menia . . . .

Sit down, Gunnar, I will tell thee, thy fair wife despairing of life. Your ship shall not be all afloat when I shall have breathed my last. Gudrun and ye shall be reconciled sooner than thou thinkest. She shall have a daughter · by the king, born to her dead husband. There shall be a maid-child born, her mother shall bear [a daughter]; she, Swanhild, shall be whiter than a sunbeam in the bright day. Thou shalt give away Gudrun to a certain good husband, a king . . . . She shall not be given away at her own pleasure; Atli, Budli's son, my brother, shall wed her. I have many things to remember of your dealings with me, how sorely ye betrayed me. I was ever joyless as long as I lived. Thou shalt desire Oddrun to wife, but Atli will not permit it. Ye shall come together in secret, she shall love thee as I ought if our destiny had been kindly decreed. Atli shall entreat you evilly, he will put you into a narrow pit of serpents. It shall not be very long afterward ere Atli shall lose his life, his happiness, and the life of his sons, for Gudrun, out of her cruel heart, shall make gory his bed with the sharp sword-edge. It had been seemlier for your sister, Gudrun . . . . the husband of her youth . . . . , if she took good counsel, or if she had a heart like mine. I have spoken many things, but she shall not . . . . lose her life. The high billows shall carry her to the heritage of Ionakr; she shall bear him heirs, sons, heirs to Ionakr. She will send Swanhild, her daughter and Sigurd's, out of the land, and Bikki's plot shall wound her, for Eormunrek shall tread her with horses. Then is all the race of Sigurd perished, and Gudrun has one sorrow more.

I will beg one boon of thee, it will be the last boon in this world. Do thou make a broad pyre on the plain, big enough to hold all of us that are going to die with Sigurd. Deck the walls of the pyre with awnings and shields, with Welsh [Gaulish] stuff well-dyed, and with Welsh . . . . Burn the Hunnish king on one side of me, and on the other side of the Hunnish king my five bondmaids decked with necklaces. Eight men-servants of noble blood, my nurse and my fosterer whom Budli gave to his child [me]. . . . Put two men at our heads and two at our feet, [two horses, two hounds,] and two hawks, so all shall be shared equally between us. Lay between us the ring-fitted sword, the iron with whetted edges; lay it again, just as when we two lay on one bed and were called by the names of man and wife. Then the ring-locked doors of Hell shall not fall on his heels; if my company follow him hence our convoy shall be no poor one, when five bondmaids follow him, eight men-servants of noble blood, my nurse, and my fosterer, whom Budli gave to his child.

Much have I spoken, but I would speak more if Fate gave me a longer time to speak in. My voice is failing me, my wounds are swelling. Nought but truth have I spoken. Now I must depart.

HELREID BRYNHILDAR (BRYNHILD'S TRIP TO HEL)

After Brynhild committed suicide on the pyre, she rode to the nether world. She met a giantess who refused her passage, but ultimately the ogress sank into the earth and Brynhild continued her journey.

II.

Brunhild, riding to Hell in her funeral chariot, encounters an Ogress.

Ogress: Thou shalt not pass my rock-supported court; it would beseem thee better to sit at the broidering, than to be in company of another's husband. Why comest thou from Welsh-land [Gaul] to my house, thou fickle being? Thou hast, lady, if thou wilt know it, . . . washed human blood off thy hands.—*Brunhild:* Blame me not, thou bride of the rock, though I were once a wicking. I shall always be held the better of us two, wherever our kindred is known.—*Ogress:* Thou wast, Brynhild, Budli's daughter, born into the world in evil hour. Thou hast destroyed the sons of Giuki, and [laid waste their good house].

Brunhild: I will tell thee a true tale out of my woe, if thou wilt know, how Giuki's heirs made me loveless and plightlorn. I lived at Heimi's in Lymdale eight years, and enjoyed life. I was twelve winters old, if thou wilt know, before I plighted my troth to any prince; they all in Lymdale called me Hild [war-goddess] the helmed, whoso knew me. Then I made the old Helm-Gunnar in Gothland go down to Hell, but gave victory to the young brother of Auda. Wodin was very wroth with me for that. He hemmed me round with shields, red and white, in Skatesholt, so that the rims of them touched; he decreed that he alone should break my sleep, who never felt fear. He let a high flame burn round my southern hall; and decreed that he alone should ride through the fire that brought me the gold that lay under Fafni. The good prince came, riding on Grani, to the hall where my foster-father lived. There he was held better than all the Danish wickings in the court. We slept and lay in one bed as if he had been my brother. Neither of us laid a hand over the other for eight nights. Gudrun, daughter of Giuki, reproached me that I slept in Sigurd's arms. It was then I knew what I would not, that they had beguiled me in my husband (*giving me a wrong one*).

Men and women shall now and always be born to live in woe. We two, Sigurd and I, shall never part again.—Sink now, Ogress!

GUDRÚNARKVIDA IN FORNA (THE OLD LAY OF GUDRUN)

This poem, laden with factual detail, was recited by Gudrun to Thjodrek at Atli's court. It takes Gudrun from the death of Sigurd to her marriage with Atli. Note that neither Atli nor Thjodrek bear any resemblance to the historical Attila and Theodoric of Verona (Dietrich von Bern in the German versions). They are simply names associated with those of famous warriors. Vigfusson and Powell have taken some liberties with the original text, which has not survived in completely intelligible condition.

Gudrun speaks: I WAS a maid of maids, my bright mother brought me up in her bower. I loved my brothers dearly, till Giuki endowed me with gold, endowed me with gold and gave me to Sigurd, till my brothers begrudged me a husband who was foremost of all. They could neither sleep nor sit in court before they put Sigurd to death.

Grani galloped from the assembly, the rattle [of his hoofs] was heard, but Sigurd himself never came back. All their horses were splashed with blood, and stained with soil beneath their riders. I went weeping to talk with Grani, with wet cheeks I asked the steed to speak. Then Grani bowed his head and sunk it in the grass; the steed knew that his master was dead. I wavered a long while, for a long while I divided my mind, before I asked the king [Gunnar] about the prince [Sigurd]. Gunnar bowed his head, but Hogni told me that Sigurd lay dead of his wounds; *saying:* 'The slayer of Gothorm lies smitten beyond the water given to the wolves. Seek thou for Sigurd in South-way. Thou shalt hear the ravens scream, the eagles scream for joy of their quarry, and the wolves howl over thy husband.'

Quoth Gudrun: Why dost thou care to talk to me so cruelly, me a desolate woman? May the ravens tear thy heart. . . . .

Hogni made answer once and no more, with an angry heart greatly moved with pity: ' Thou wilt have more still to weep over, Gudrun, if the ravens tear my heart.'

I turned away from our talk into the heritage of the wide-roving wolves [forest]. The night seemed moonless [pitch-black] to me, as I sat sorrow-stricken over Sigurd. The wolves howled on all sides . . . . [would they had devoured me, and] the bears had gnawed me to pieces as they do the young sap-shoots of the birch. I wandered over the mountain five whole days told, before I lit on Half's high hall. I stayed with Thora, Hakon's daughter, in Denmark, seven seasons [years]. She embroidered in gold, to please me, southern halls and Danish swans. We had on our rolls the play of warriors [i. e. pictures of battles wrought in needlework], and on our handiwork the king's thanes, the red shield, the Hunnish warriors, a sworded company, a helmed company, the king's guards. Sigmund's ships were gliding from the shore, with gilt figure-heads and carved bows. We broidered on our broidery how Sigar and Siggeir fought south in Fife.

But now Grimhild, the Gothic lady, heard where I was living, in a friend's dwelling. She asked my brothers, her sons, holding a parley with them, asking over and over again if they would recompense their sister for her son, or pay her weregild for her slain husband. Gunnar said that he was willing to offer gold to recompense her claim, and Hogni said the same. Moreover, she asked who would go to saddle the war-horse, to horse the wagons, ride the steed, fly the hawk, shoot arrows out of the yew bow. . . . .

Three kings came before my knees: Waldar of the Danes and Iarisleif . . . . Eymund was the third of them, and Iariscar: in they came like kings, the company of the Lombards; they wore red fur, variegated mail-coats, enamelled helmets, were girt with short swords, had brown hair cut across their brows. Each of them would gladly give me choice gifts, yea, choice gifts, and speak lovingly to me, to try and make me comforted . . . . but I would not put my trust in them . . . . ere she herself [my mother Grimhild] called on me to speak my mind, *saying*: ' I give thee gold to take, Gudrun, plenty of all wealth, thy dead father's heritage, red rings, Lothwy's hall, all the hall-hangings the fallen king left, Hunnish maidens that can weave checkered linen and work beautifully in gold, so that it shall please thee; thou shalt have all Budli's wealth for thine own, thou shalt be endowed with gold and given to Atli.'—*Then I answered*: I will not have him for husband, nor wed the brother of Brunhild; it beseems me not to have children by the son of Budli, or live with him. — *Grimhild answered*: Do not thou entertain hatred against the kings [thy brothers and Atli], albeit we were the first to begin it. Do thou rather, when thou bringest up thy sons, make as if Sigurd and Sigmund were yet alive.—*Then I said*: I cannot make merry, Grimhild, nor plight my faith to the hero [Atli], since the greedy corse-harpies drunk the heart's blood of Sigurd together.—*Grimhild answered*: He is the best-born of all kings I have known, and the boldest of heroes. Him thou shalt wed, or else be husbandless until old age overcomes thee, save thou take him.—*I said*: Do not continue to thrust upon me, with importunity, that cursed race. He shall [one day] deal a deadly blow to Gunnar, and cut the heart out of Hogni, and I shall never rest till I have taken his life in the prime. Then Grimhild, weeping, broke in upon her words, when she [Gudrun] foretold ills to come upon her [Grimhild's] sons, and sore affliction to her offspring.—*Quoth Grimhild*: I will give thee yet more lands and servants, Wincrag, Walcrag, if thou wilt take them; keep them all thy life and rejoice in them, daughter.—*Then I said*: I will not choose him among kings, nor have him thrust upon me, among all his kin. A husband will bring me no joy, nor will he, that shall be the death of my brothers, be a shelter to my sons.

But Grimhild brought me a beaker of drink, cold and bitter, whereby I forgot my wrongs. It was blent with the might of the earth, with ice-cold sea-water, and with the blood of sacrifice. On this horn there was every kind of letter engraved and painted in red (I could not read them), long ling-fishes [snakes], and unreaped corn ears 'from the land of Harding [the under-world],' and the guts of beasts. In this beer there were many evil spells mixed, ... and hearth's soot, the inner parts of beasts slain in sacrifice, boiled hog's liver because it allays strife. . . .

Then every hero was seen on his horse, and the Gaulish wives lifted up on the wagons. We rode seven days over the cold land, and seven days more we worked our way over the waves, and the third seven days we went upon the dry land. The warders of the lofty forts opened the gates when we rode into the court . . . . (*rest missing*).

GUDRÚNARKVIDA IN THRIDJA (THE THIRD LAY OF GUDRUN)

In this short poem, obviously a fragment, Gudrun proved her innocence through ordeal. She had been accused by Herkja, Atli's concubine, of adultery with Thjodrek.

Quoth Gudrun: How goes it with thee ever now, Atli, thou son of Budli? Art thou heavy of heart? thou never laughest! Thy gentlemen would be better pleased if thou wouldst talk with men and look upon me.—*Quoth Atli:* This is my grief, Gudrun, thou daughter of Giuki. Herkia told me in the hall that thou and Theodric had slept under one roof, and lightly spread one bed for the twain of you.— *Quoth Gudrun:* I will take an oath about all this matter, upon the white holy stone, that I have never dealt with the son of Theodmar as man and wife are wont, save that once I fell upon the neck of the king of hosts, the blameless prince,—and no more embraces had we,—as we twain bowed our heads together as we talked of our woes. Theodric came here with thirty men, no one of those thirty men is left. I am bereft of my brothers and of my young son, I am bereft of all my next of kin. Now do thou send to Saxi, the lord of the Southerners, he knows how to hallow the boiling cauldron.

Seven hundred men came into the hall to see the king's wife deal with the cauldron.

Quoth Gudrun: Gunnar shall not come, I shall not call Hogni, I shall never see my sweet brothers more. Hogni would have avenged me of this foul charge with the sword, but now I must clear myself of this charge with my own hand.

She dipped her white hand to the bottom [of the cauldron] and took out the precious stones. 'See now, men, how the cauldron boils! I am proved guiltless according to the holy custom.' Atli's heart laughed in his breast when he saw Gudrun's hands whole. 'Now Herkia must go to the cauldron, she that imputed guilt to Gudrun.'

He has never seen a pitiful sight that did not see how Herkia's hands were scalded that day. They led the maid to a foul slough.

Poet's Epilogue: Thus was Gudrun proved guiltless of the foul charge.

ODDRÚNARGRÁTR (THE DIRGE OF ODDRUN)

Oddrun, Atli's sister, described her unfortunate passion for Gunnar.
Here was one more reason for Atli's hatred of the scion of the Gjukungs.

IN stories of old I heard tell how a maid came to Morn-land.
Heidrek's daughter [Borgny] could get no help on earth [in her
labour]. Ordrun, Atli's sister, heard that the maiden was in sore
labour; she took the bitted steed from its stall, and set the saddle upon
the black charger. She rode her horse through the flat paths of earth,
till she came to the high-towering hall. She swept the saddle off the
slender steed, and went in up the hall and spake this first of all: 'What
is the last news in this land, and what is the . . . . in Hunland?'
   The Bondmaid answers: Borgny, thy friend, lies here overcome with
the throes of labour. Ordrun, see if thou canst help her.—*Ordrun
answers:* Who has brought this dishonour on her? Why have the
sharp pains come upon Borgny?—*Bondwoman:* Wilmund the hero is his
name, he lay with the maid five nights, and she hid it from her father.
   They spake no more then I think, but the gentle lady went in to
sit before the maiden's knees [that is, to act as midwife to Borgny].
Mightily chanted Ordrun, powerfully chanted Ordrun keen charms over
Borgny. . . . . *The child is born.* Then the labouring lady began to speak;
these were the first words she said: 'May the gracious powers, Frigg
and Freyja, and many other divinities, help thee as thou deliverest me
from my labour!'—*Ordrun:* 'I did not bend to help thee because . . . .
I vowed, and I fulfilled what I spoke, that ever I should render help,
whereso.' . . . .
   Borgny: Thou art surely distraught, Ordrun, and beside thy wit, to
speak so many hard words to me, [*her words must have been in the preced-
ing blank.*] But I was wont to follow thee over the earth, as if we had
been born of two brothers.—*Ordrun:* I remember what thou saidst
one evening to me when I took Gunnar to my bed. Thou didst say
that such misfortune would never befall any maid but me.
   Then the sorrow-stricken maid [Ordrun] sat her down and began
to tell over the tale of her wrongs and woes. 'I was bred up in
a king's hall with every bliss, as men say. I enjoyed my life and the
wealth of my father for five winters, as long as my father was alive.
It was the last word he spoke, that stern king, ere he sunk in death.
He bade them endow me with red gold, and send me south as wife
to Grimhild's son [Gunnar], and build a castle for Brunhild, saying
that she should be a wish maid [to be wooed for], for he said that
no maid more renowned than she should ever be brought up on earth,
save the Judge [Fate] cut her life short. Brunhild wrought at the

broidery in the bower, she had [a wall of flame] about her, the earth quaked and the heavens above when Fafni's slayer sought out the stronghold. Then a fight was fought with the Welsh sword [from Gaul], and the stronghold of Brunhild was broken. It did not last long, but a short space only before she knew all the wiles [*that she had been deceived by Sigurd*]. She wreaked a dire revenge for all this, of which we have proofs enough. It shall go forth through all lands how she let herself die with Sigurd. But I loved King Gunnar, as Brunhild should have loved him. They offered Atli, my brother, red rings enough and no small ransom. He [Gunnar] offered fifteen homesteads for me, and the burthen of Grani, if he [Atli] would take it. But Atli said that he would never take the bride-fee from a son of Giuki. Albeit we could not withstand our love, nor deny my promise [*of Love*] to the King [Gunnar]. Many of my kinsmen bore witness that they had found us two together, but Atli said that I should never devise any wrong-doing or dishonour; yet no man should speak words of denial on another's behalf, in a matter of love. Atli sent his messengers through Mirkwood to prove me, and they came where they should not have come, when we lay in one sheet together. We offered them red rings not to tell Atli thereof, but they hastened home forthwith and told it eagerly to Atli. . . . *Atli and his men thereupon devise a plot to avenge his Sister's dishonour upon Gunnar*, but they hid it [the treachery] from Gudrun, who should have been the first to know it.

There was a clattering of gold hoofs to be heard when the Heirs of Giuki rode into the courtyard. They cut the heart out of Hogni, but put his brother in the pit of snakes. The good king began to strike the harp, for the noble king thought that I should come to his help. At that very hour I was away at Geirmund's at a banquet. I began to hear as far as Hlessey how the strings rang amain. I bade my bondmaids to make ready, I wished to save the king's life. We ferried over the Sound until we saw the halls of Atli. Then there came speeding out the accursed [snake-dam],—may she pine away!—and she pierced to Gunnar's heart, so that I could not save the famous king.

ATLIKVIDA (THE LAY OF ATLI)

This account of the deaths of Gunnar and Hogni is one of the oldest poems in the Poetic Edda. Here we see the heathen Gudrun avenging the death of her brothers on her barbarous spouse Atli. She is vastly different from the Christian Kriemhild of the Nibelungenlied who was loyal to her murdered husband even to the extent of destroying her brothers. Like Medea, Gudrun is the barbarian woman, intent on the destruction of the man who used her love for his purposes and destroyed her kin. The bereft Andromache or Electra or even the earlier Gudrun held their grief in silence.

IN the olden days Atli sent one of his trusty warriors, whose name was Knefred, to Gunnar. He came to the courts of Giuki, to the hall of Gunnar, with its hearth-compassing benches, and to the sweet ale. The henchmen were drinking wine in the great Hall, the strangers kept silence, for they feared the wrath of the Hniflungs; till Knefred the Southern messenger cried with an evil voice from where he sat on the high bench:—

'Atli hath sent me hither on the bridled steed through the wild Mirkwood to ride his errand, to bid you, Gunnar, to come to the hearth-compassing benches . . . to visit Atli. Ye shall choose you gifts there, shields and smooth-shaven shafts, gold-red helms and Hunnish maidens, silver-gilt saddle-cloths and crimson shirts, . . . darts and bridled chargers. He says that he will give you the wide field of Gnite-heath, and store of sounding spears and gilt shields, huge treasure, and the dwellings of Danp, and the famous forest men call Mirkwood.'

Then Gunnar turned his head, and spake to Hogni: 'What counsel dost thou give us respecting all this that we hear, thou young hero? I know no gold on Gnite-heath, but that we have as much again. We have seven treasuries full of swords, every one of them with a golden hilt. My steed is the best, my brand the keenest, my bow the best strung, my mail-coat is of gold, my helm and shield are the whitest, they came from the hall of Kiar. My harness alone is better than that of all the Huns.'

Then spake Hogni . . .: 'What thinkest thou the lady [our sister] meant, when she sent us a ring wrapt in the coat of the beast of the heath? I think that she gave us a warning thereby. For I have found wolf's hair twisted about the red ring. Our way will be wolfish [murderous] if we ride on this errand.'

It was neither his friends nor his neighbours, nor his wise men, nor his counsellors, nor his mighty men that made Gunnar eager to go.

Up spake Gunnar, as beseems a king, gallantly in his mead-hall, out of the pride of his heart—'Rise up, Fiornir [my cupbearer], let the

94

gold-ringed cups pass round the benches from hand to hand. The wolf, that old grey-coated beast, shall rule over the heritage (Hoard) of the Hniflungs, if Gunnar perish. The bears with black hide shall bite with fierce teeth at the "gold" if Gunnar come back no more.'

The blameless warriors wept as they led the warlike kings out of the courts of the Hniflungs [to bid them farewell]. Then spake Hogni's young heir: 'Fare hale and hearty wherever your hearts list to go.'

The gallant kings made their bridled steeds gallop apace over the mountains and through the wild Mirkwood. All Hunmark shook where the strong heroes passed, they rode their chargers through the . . . green mantled fields.

II.

They reach Atli's Palace . . . darts, where Atli was drinking wine in the great hall. The warders were sitting without, to guard it from Gunnar, if he and his brother should come thither to waken the [fierce] battle with the sounding spears.

Their sister met her two brothers at once as they came into the hall, . . . 'Thou art betrayed, Gunnar (*she said*), how wilt thou, O King, withstand the treacherous wiles of the Huns? Get thee out of the hall as fast as thou mayst. Thou hadst better not have come hither, brother, to the . . . hearth - compassing benches to visit Atli's hall. Thou shouldst be sitting in the saddle through the sunlit day, making the Fates to weep over the death-pale corses, and making the Hunnish amazons to know the harrow, and setting Atli himself in the pit of serpents—but now that serpent-pit is dug for thee.'

Then answered Gunnar, the Hniflung hero: 'It is too late, sister, to call up the Hniflungs; it is too far to get their help, my blameless champions, across the "craggy" mountains of the Rhine.'

They took Gunnar, the friend of the Burgundians, and set him in fetters and bound him fast. Hogni cut down seven men with his keen sword, and cast the eighth into the hot fire. So should a brave man defend himself against his foes ! . . .

They asked the brave King of the Goths if he would buy his life with gold. [Then said Gunnar] 'Hogni's bleeding heart must be laid in my hand, carved with the keen-cutting knife out of the breast of the good knight.'

They carved the heart of Hialli (the thrall) from out his breast, and laid it bleeding on a charger, and bore it to Gunnar.

Then spake Gunnar, king of men: 'Here I have the heart of Hialli the coward, unlike to the heart of Hogni the brave. It quakes greatly as it lies on the charger, but it quaked twice as much when it lay in his breast.'

Hogni laughed when they cut out the quick heart of that crested hero, he had little thought of whimpering. They laid it bleeding on the charger, and bore it before Gunnar.

Then spake Gunnar, the Hniflungs' hero: 'Here I have the heart of Hogni the brave, unlike to the heart of Hialli the coward; it quakes very little as it lies on the charger; but it quaked far less when it lay in his breast. May thou ever be as far from joy [luck], Atli, as thou art from the hope of the treasures! for the whole Hoard of the Hniflungs

95

is hidden with me alone now that Hogni is dead. While we two were alive I always had a doubt, I have none now that I alone am alive. The Rhine, the stream the gods know well, shall possess the strife-begetting Treasure of the heroes, the heritage of the Hniflungs. The great rings shall gleam in the rolling waters rather than they shall shine on the hands of the sons of the Huns.'

*   *   *   *   *   *   *   *

Quoth Atli, ' Harness the wheel-wain, the prisoner lies in bonds.'

[*Some corrupt lines, which cannot be translated, come in here ; the sense of them is that Gudrun tries to dissuade her husband from putting her brother to death and so breaking the oath he had sworn to him, saying :—*]

' May it be with thee, Atli, according to the oaths, which thou didst oftentimes swear to Gunnar, calling aged witnesses to hear thy vow, by the southing sun, and the Great God's rock, and by the lintels of thy bedchamber, and by the ring of Wuldor. . . .'

The band of warriors put the king alive into the pit that was crawling with serpents. But Gunnar, alone there, in his wrath smote the harp with his hands; the strings rang out. So should a valiant hero keep his gold from his foes.

III.

Atli made his steed gallop back from the murder toward his own land. There was a din in the courtyard, crowded with horses, the clang of men's weapons, when they came back from the heath.

Then Gudrun came out to meet Atli with a gilt chalice. . . . 'Take, lord, in thine hall from Gudrun. . . .'

Heavy with wine Atli's ale-beakers rang when the Huns gathered 'in the hall, when the long-bearded heroes assembled together.

The bright-faced [Gudrun], that fierce lady, hastened to bear the wine to the lords, and in her cruelty to share out the dainty morsels to the pale-faced princes, but to Atli she spake a word of mockery. ' Thou hast eaten the fresh-bleeding hearts of thy sons, mixed with honey, thou giver of swords. Now thou shalt digest the gory flesh of man, thou stern king, having eaten of it as a dainty morsel, and sent it as a mess to thy friends. Never more shalt thou, merry with ale, call thy two sons Erp and Eitil to thy knees from thy high seat. Thou shalt never see in the midst of thy court the young princes shafting their spears, clipping their horses' manes, or spurring their steeds.'

Then arose a hum on the benches, a horrible murmur from the men, uproar among them that were in fine raiment, the children of the Huns weeping aloud—save Gudrun only, she never wept for her bear-hearted brothers or her sweet sons, the young innocents that she bore to Atli.

The swan-white queen strewed gold abroad, and bribed the household with red rings,—making doom to wax high,—and poured out the bright hoards; she grudged not the treasures. . . .

Merry was Atli, he had drunk himself mad, weapon he had none, he was not wary against Gudrun. It had been often a sweeter play between them when they embraced each other before the princes.

With the point of the sword she gave the bed blood to drink with her murderous hand, and loosed the hounds. She cast the hot brand against the door of the hall. . . . This is the weregild she got for her brothers. To the flame she gave all that were in the hall, that had come from Mirkwood from the murder of Gunnar. The old timbers fell down; the treasure-houses smoked; the king's houses and the amazons within them sunk life-lorn into the burning fire.

It is told to the end. Never has other lady gone forth in mail to avenge her brothers as she [Gudrun] did. The fair queen wrought the death of three great kings before she died!

ATLAMÁL IN GROENLENZKA (THE GREENLAND LAY OF ATLI)

Later than the older Atlikvida, with which this Greenlandish poet is obviously acquainted, this poem is considerably more stylized from a literary standpoint. The rich, partially technical vocabulary of the original text cannot easily be reproduced in this translation or any other. Nevertheless, the characters of Gudrun and Atli are as sharply delineated as those of the most sophisticated characters of any period of literature.

MEN have heard the dreadful tale, how the heroes held a parley together—good to nobody; they held a secret meeting, whence came woe upon themselves, and also to the sons of Giuki who were betrayed. The Norns let their doom wax high, since they were doomed to die. Atli took an evil step although he was a wise man; he hewed down a mighty pillar and did himself great harm, when he sent off his messengers to bid his brothers-in-law seek him without tarrying. The goodwife was brave, she used her wit, she caught the drift of the words which they were speaking in secret. The wise lady was hard put to it, she desired to help them, but they must cross the sea, and she herself could not come, so she graved runes; but Wingi—bent on treason was he—put them wrong ere he gave them [to her brethren].

Forth went the messengers of Atli and crossed Lim-firth, where the princes dwelt. They were merry with wine and kindled the fires—they thought not on guile—when the messengers came. They took the gifts their sister had sent them, and hung them on the pillars, they thought them of no moment. Then came Kostbera,—she was Hogni's wife,— a most merry lady, and greeted both the brethren. And Glaumvor, Gunnar's wife, was glad also. She never lacked sure wisdom, she busied herself with the needs of the guests. They [Wingi and his fellow] begged Hogni to come, that Gunnar might be more willing to come— the treachery was clear, if they had but paid heed to it. Then Gunnar asked if Hogni would go. Hogni said that he would stand by the other's will.

The ladies served the mead; there was store of all good cheer; they bore drink-horns a many, till men had drunk their fill. The two [Hogni and his wife] went to rest as seemed good to them. Kostbera the kindly, she knew how to read runes; she read through the letters by the light of the fire, she kept guard on her tongue between her teeth; the letters were so dark that it was hard to read. Then she and Hogni went to bed. The gentle lady had a dream—she hid it not, but told it to her husband as soon as she awoke. 'Thou art going away from home, Hogni, take heed to what thou doest. Few men weigh what is before them; go this journey another time. I have read the runes thy sister

98

engraved, she has not bidden thee to her this time. And I wonder at one thing, and cannot make it out, how it came about that she cut them wrong, for there were hints therein as if the death of you both were awaiting you if you go now; either she missed a letter or another has put them wrong.'—*Quoth Hogni* : . . . . The king [Atli] will endow us with ember-red gold. I am never in doubt, though I do hear any rumour of ill.—*Quoth Kostbera* : It shall be ill with you if ye go thither now, it will not be a friendly meeting this time. I dreamed, Hogni,—I will not hide it,—that it will go hard with you, and I fear it will be so. I thought thy sheets were burning in the fire, and that a high flame was showering sparks through thy house.—*Quoth Hogni* : Here lie linen rags cast off, they will soon be burnt, and they are the sheets thou sawest in thy dream.—*Quoth Kostbera* : I saw a bear come in and tear up the seat-pillars, he shook his paws so that we were frightened. He held many of us in his mouth so that we could do nothing, there was no small trampling there too.—*Quoth Hogni* : The weather shall wax and soon grow to a gale; thou didst dream of a white bear, that means a snow-storm from the east.—*Quoth Kostbera* : I dreamed that an eagle flew in, all up the hall, spattering us all with blood, that will certainly bring us ill. I saw from his fierceness that it was the fetch of Atli.—*Quoth Hogni* : We shall make a big slaughter; then we shall see blood; it often means oxen when we dream of eagles. Atli's heart is single whatsoever thou dream.

Then they ceased. Every speech comes to an end.

The well-born [king Gunnar and Gleamwor] awakened, it was the same story with them. Gleamwor said that she had had evil dreams . . . . warning Gunnar not to go.—*Quoth Gleamwor* : I dreamed of a gallows set up, and that thou wast going to be hanged thereon. I saw thee eaten alive of serpents, so that I lost thee. There came the crack of doom. Tell me what it means.—*Quoth Gunnar* : (Answer lost.)—*Quoth Gleamwor* : I saw a bloody blade drawn out of thy shirt. It is hard to have to tell such dream to a husband. I thought I saw a spear smitten through thy body, while the wolves howled at either side.—*Quoth Gunnar* : It was curs running, barking very sharply. The flight of spears often means dogs' baying.—*Quoth Gleamwor* : I thought I saw a river rushing up the hall; it roared with fury, dashing over the benches, and broke the legs of both of you brothers; the water was pitiless. That must mean something.—*Quoth Gunnar* : There corn-fields shall be waving where thou sawest a river; the awns catch our feet when we walk through a field.—*Quoth Gleamwor* : I thought I saw dead women, poorly clad, come in here to-night; they wished to choose thee, and bade thee come to their hall without tarrying. I fear thy good fairies have dropped away from thee.—*Quoth Gunnar* : It is too late to talk; now it is settled, we cannot escape our doom. We are bound to go now, yea, though it is not unlikely that our lives may be short.

When the dawning showed they all arose and made them ready, but their wives would have held them back. They went forth five together, and twice as many henchmen—it was ill devised :—*they two;* Snowar and Solar, Hogni's sons; and Orkning was the name of the last, this blithe hero was Gleamwor's brother. The fair-clad ladies went with them till the firth parted them; they would alway have held them back, but they were the more bent on going. Then Gleamwor, whom Gunnar wed, began to speak, talking to Wingi as she thought best: 'I know not whether ye will reward us according to our desert. It is foul shame to the guest if any ill happens through him [to the host].' Then Wingi swore, he did not spare himself: 'May the giants take me if I lie to you; may the gallows have me body and bones if I thought on any breach of faith.'

Bera blithe-hearted began to speak: 'Sail in safety, and speed ye well! May ye fare as I wish you . . . .' Lovingly Hogni answered his wife: 'Comfort you, gallant ladies, whatsoever betide . . . .' Then they kissed each other ere they turned away; their fates lay apart when their ways parted.

They began to row amain, ... keel . . . .; they bent full on their backs, they waxed very furious, the oar-thongs split, the tholes broke. They did not moor the boat before they turned away. I must tell all to the end—they could see the hall that Budli owned standing a little farther on. The gate-bars creaked when Hogni shook it.

Up spake Wingi then, he had best held his peace : 'Keep off from the house, ye may look for an ill welcome. I shall soon see you burnt, ye shall soon be slaughtered. With fair words I prayed you to come here, but there was falsehood beneath them. Get you gone, unless ye be willing to wait till I cut you a gallows.'—Up spake Hogni, he had no thought of yielding, he feared nothing that might befall: 'Never think to frighten us! Thou wilt not! If thou speak another word it will be the worse for thee.'

They thrust at Wingi and smote him to death, they hewed at him with their axes while the breath rattled in his throat.

Atli's men gathered, and did on their mail-coats; they marched in such wise that the wall was between them. They began to shout to one another, all in wrath together.

Quoth Atli : 'We had settled beforehand to take your lives!'—*Quoth Hogni:* 'It looks little as if ye settled it beforehand, ye are still unready, and we have slain one of you, smitten him to death; he was one of your host.' They waxed wroth when they heard those words, they put forth their fingers and took hold on the strings, they shot sharply forth, covering themselves with their shields.

With that there came a message into the hall that told what was doing outside; they heard a thrall shouting loudly without: . . . Gudrun was roused when she heard this bad news; she was laden with necklaces, she tore them all away, she flung the silver down so that every link was snapped asunder. She went out of the hall forthwith; it was not softly that she threw back the doors, it was in no fearful mood that she went out to welcome the new comers. She turned to the Hniflungs—it was their last greeting, and there was earnest in it; moreover, she said, 'I tried to save you and keep you at home, and yet ye are here. No man can fly from fate.' She spake wisely, trying to make peace, but they would not be counselled [or accede to it], all of them said No. When the high-born lady saw that the game was a bloody one, she hardened her heart, and threw off her mantle, took a naked sword in her hand and fought for the life of her kinsmen. She was no weakling in the fight, wherever her hand fell ; Giuki's daughter struck down two warriors. She smote Atli's brother .... she shaped her stroke so that she smote off his foot, and struck down the other so that he never rose again, sending him to hell. Her hand faltered not.

The fight they fought, it was famed far and wide; it was greater than all the other feats of the children of Giuki. It is said that the Hniflungs, as long as they were alive unwounded, never ceased to deal blows with their swords, riving mail-coats and hewing through helmets, as their hearts bade them. They fought all through the morning, through the first watches and the forenoon till mid-day was past—less would be a good fight—the field was a-swim with blood. The two sons of Bera and her brother slew eighteen. They were the victors.

The hero [Atli] broke into speech, though he was very wroth : ' It is ill to look on, it is your doing; we were thirty fighting men, but eleven of us are left alive; we are as a remnant from the fire. We were five brethren when Budli died. Hell holds half of us now; two lie smitten down. I made a hard match—it cannot be gainsaid—thou woeful woman, I have little comfort from thee. I have never had rest since thou camest into my hands; thou hast bereft me of my kindred, defrauded me of my wealth, sent my sister to death. Needs must I feel it sorely.'—*Quoth Gudrun :* Speakest thou so, Atli, yet thou didst begin it. Thou tookest my mother and murdered her for her riches; my sweet cousin thou didst starve in a cave. It is a laughter to me, that thou talkest of thy wrongs. I thank the Gods that thou farest ill.— *Quoth Atli :* Now I rouse you all, my men, to heap up hurt on this proud wife of mine; I would fain see it. Do your best to draw tears from Gudrun. I would gladly see her in distress. Take Hogni, and flesh him with a knife, cut out his heart, make you ready! As for the fierce Gunnar, tie him up to the gallows; be not afraid; call the snakes to their meal!

Quoth Hogni : Do thy will, I shall gladly endure it; I shall prove myself steadfast; I have been tried more sorely. Ye were shamefully beaten as long as we were sound, now we are so wounded thou must have thy way.....

Then said Beiti, Atli's steward: 'Let us take Hialli and spare Hogni. Let us do half the work only. Hialli is only fit to die, however long he live he will always be known as a good-for-nothing.' The kettle-keeper was sore afraid, he did not wait, [but ran away and] fell to whimpering, and hid away in every corner he could find, crying that it was a woeful battle indeed if he were to pay for all the hurt done, and a black day when he must die and leave his swine, and all the good fare that he had had. But they took Budli's cook and lifted up the knife; the coward thrall cried out before he felt the blade, praying them to spare him; he said that he would be glad if his life were but left him to dung the field, to do the meanest work, if only he might live.

Hogni heard this; few would have done as he did, plead for the thrall that they would let him go: ' It would trouble me less to play out the play, why should we be made to listen to this screeching?' Then they laid hands on the hero; there was no further choice for them to put it off any more. And Hogni laughed, the henchman heard it; he knew how to bear it, he suffered the torture bravely.

Gunnar took a harp and struck it with his toes, he knew how to play, so that the ladies wept and the men fell a weeping when they heard it. .... The stronger had his way, the rafters burst asunder! ....
When he died the day was yet young. .....

Atli thought much of this, that he had overcome them both; he spake to the gallant lady and spared not to taunt her: 'It is still morning and thou hast lost both of those thou lovedst. Much of what has happened is thine own doing.'—*Quoth Gudrun :* Thou art merry, Atli, giving notice of thy murders. Yet shalt thou rue it if thou try it to the end. A heritage of woe shall remain, I tell thee verily, which will always go ill with thee as long as I live.—*Quoth Atli :* I will traverse that, I can see another way, better by half. Let us not throw away our good luck: I will atone to thee with gifts of slaves, and costly treasures, and snow-white silver to thy heart's content.—*Quoth Gudrun :* There is no hope of that. I refuse it. I have broken atonements where there was less cause. I was always thought hard to deal with, but now I shall be so; I could put up with everything as long as Hogni was alive. We were brought up in one house, we have played many a play together, we grew up together in the Grove. Grimhild used to deck us with gold and necklaces. Thou canst never recompense me for my brothers' death, nor do anything to please me. Men's tyranny often over-rides women's wishes. The king is mated if the pawns are taken. The tree must fall if the roots be cut; thou shalt have thine own way now, Atli.

The king believed her, through his over-foolishness, yet the treachery was easy to see if he had paid heed withal. Gudrun was crafty, she knew how to dissemble; she made as if she took it lightly, she played a double game.

They ceased speaking, the banquet was prepared; she made a banquet of ale for the funeral of her brothers, and Atli one for his men. This feast was uproarious; her heart was hardened, she waged war against the race of Budli. She planned too great a vengeance on her husband.

She called to her children that were tottering about the pillars of the seats, the fierce boys whimpered but they did not weep, they went to their mother's arms and asked her what she wanted.—*Quoth Gudrun :* Do not ask me, I mean to kill you both. I have long meant to save you from old age. [The bearing of the boys' answer not clear.] Try to give rest to thy anger for a little while. The passionate woman slew the two brothers in their childhood—an evil deed it was—she cut both their throats.

But Atli asked where the boys had gone to play, since he saw them not.—*Gudrun answered :* I will tell thee a thing, Atli, that passes all others; I will not hide it from thee. Thy joy shall be minished, Atli, when thou hast heard it all. Thou didst waken no small woes when thou slewest my brethren. I have slept little since they fell. I promised thee evil, I gave thee full warning. It was in the morning that thou didst speak to me, I remember it well [of my brother's death], now it is evening and it is thy turn to give ear. Thou hast lost thy sons in the worst of ways! know that their skulls have been used as ale-cups. I eked out thy drink, I mixed it with blood, I took their

102

hearts and roasted them on the spits, and gave them to thee, telling thee they were calves' hearts. Thou atest them up all, leaving nought; thou didst mumble them greedily, trusting in thy teeth. Thou hast eaten thine own children, the worst fate a man can have. It was my doing, yet I do not boast thereof.—*Atli said:* Cruel indeed thou wast, Gudrun, to do such a deed as to mix my children's blood with my drink. Thou hast slain thine own children, the worst thing thou couldst do; thou leavest me no peace, evil follows evil. — *Quoth Gudrun:* I am minded to do more, to slay thee also. One cannot do too much harm to such a king as thou art. Thou hast done deeds such as none have ever done, foolish cruelties in this house; and now thou hast added to it as I have lately heard, falling into great crimes. Thou hast drunk thine own funeral feast.—*Quoth Atli:* Thou shalt be burnt on a pyre, and stoned to death. Then thou shalt have earned that which thou hast always been seeking.—*Quoth Gudrun:* Tell to-morrow such prophecies of thyself. I am minded through a seemlier death to pass into another light.

They sat in the same chamber, each bearing a deep grudge against the other, bandying words of hate; neither of them was happy. The Hniflung's [Hogni's son's] wrath waxed high, he planned a mighty revenge, telling Gudrun of his hate for Atli. She remembered how they had dealt with Hogni; she said that she should be happy if she could revenge his father. Within a little space Atli was smitten. Hogni's son and Gudrun herself smote him.

The king broke into speech; starting from his sleep, he felt his wound and said that he was past need of bandages: 'Tell me the whole truth, who has smitten the son of Budli. I have been hardly dealt with, I have no hope of life.'—*Quoth Gudrun:* Grimhild's daughter will not lie to thee. It was my doing that thy life is fleeting, and the doing of Hogni's son that thy wounds overcome thee. — *Quoth Atli:* Ye have made haste to slay, though it was wrong of you; it is ill to betray the friend that trusted in thee. I left my home in love to woo thee, Gudrun; thou wast praised in thy widowhood, and renowned for thy pride; it has turned out no lie now that it has come to the proof. Thou didst come home hither and a host of men with us, our company was altogether glorious; there was a mighty show of noble men, store of cattle, and we had great pleasure therein, there was wealth of money, and many took share thereof. I paid thee the bride-price, abundance of treasure, thirty thralls, seven good bondmaids,—that was an honour to thee,—and silver to boot; but thou didst take all this as if it were nought, unless thou shouldst rule over the land which Budli left me. Thou didst plot [under mine]. . . . Thou didst make thy mother-in-law to sit oft-times in tears. I never found any household at peace since thy coming.

Quoth Gudrun: Thou liest now, Atli, though I reck little thereof. I was seldom easy to deal with, but thou didst magnify my wrath. Ye young brethren fought with one another, strife arose between you, the half of thy house went to hell thereby; all that should have been peaceful quivered with hate. We were three, brothers and sisters, deemed unyielding; we went abroad and followed Sigurd, we roved about, every one steering his own ship; we set forth to seek adventures, until we came to the east [here]. Before that we slew kings, and divided their lands; the nobles did homage to us, in token of their terror of us. We inlawed by force those whom we would justify, and filled him that had nought with good things. When the Hunnish king [Sigurd] died, our glory departed in a moment. Sore grief was mine to be called a widow, bitter pain to me to come into Atli's household. A champion was my first husband, his loss was ill to bear; but thou, as far as I know, never camest from the Court, whether thou wast pleading thy suit or sitting on the suit of another—thou couldst never carry it, or hold thine own..... —*Quoth Atli:* Thou liest, Gudrun, there is little to choose between our lots, our lives now are maimed altogether. But I pray thee, Gudrun, entreat me honourably when they bear me out [to bury me].—*Quoth Gudrun:* I will buy thee a ship and a stained coffin, I will wax the sheet well that shall shroud thy body, and provide all that is needful, as if we had loved one another.

Now Atli became a corpse; the grief of kinsmen was great; the high-born lady fulfilled all that she had promised. The wise Gudrun tried to slay herself, but she was respited; she died another time.

Poet's Epilogue: Happy is he that shall beget such a bold lady as Giuki begat. The TALE of their QUARREL [Gudrun's and Atli's] shall live after them, in every land, wheresoever men hear it told.

TREGROF GUDRÚNAR (GUDRUN'S CHAIN OF WOES)

Soon after Sigurd died, Gudrun bore a daughter, Swanhild. After Atli's death Gudrun became the wife of King Jonaker, to whom she bore three sons, Sorli, Erp, and Hamdir. Jonaker also adopted Swanhild, the fame of whose beauty spread even to what is now the Ukraine. The Gothic king of those parts, Ermanarich, sought her hand, but, according to Jordanes, sixth century historian of the Ostrogoths, he had her (Sunilla) trampled to death by wild horses. Jordanes says her brothers, Ammius (Hamdir) and Surus (Sorli) avenged her. With the death of Gudrun's last children, the curse of Andvari had run its course.

First four lines cannot be translated. Subject: The pyre is being reared in the court (tá).

GUDRUN, Giuki's daughter, sat weeping in the court; she [began sorrowfully to number her woes], and with tearful cheeks to tell over her sorrows in manifold ways.

I have known three fires, three hearths; I have been carried to the houses of three husbands. The first was Sigurd, the best of them all, whom my brothers did to death. I neither saw nor knew . . . . I thought it a still harder trouble when they gave me to Atli. [I called my brave little sons apart to talk with me. I could find no recompense for my wrongs till I cut off the heads of the Hniflungs.]

I went down to the strand; angry with the Fates I was, [I wished to defy their hateful curse]; but the high waves bore me up without drowning me. I reached the land, for I was fated to live.

I went for the third time to the bed of a mighty king, hoping for better fate, and I bore children, sons, . . . to Ionakr. But the bondmaids sat round Swanhild, whom I loved best of my children; she was like a glorious sunbeam in my bower. I endowed her with gold and goodly raiment before I married her into Gothland. That was the hardest of all my sorrows, when they trod Swanhild's fair hair in the dust under the hoofs of the horses: but the sorest when they slew my Sigurd, robbed of his victories, in my bed: and the cruellest when the fierce snakes pierced Gunnar to the heart: and the sharpest when they cut Hogni the hero to the heart, while he was yet alive. I can remember many woes. Harness, Sigurd, thy white steed; let thy fleet horse gallop hither, for here sits neither daughter-in-law, nor daughter, to give gifts to me. Remember, Sigurd, what we promised one another when we both went into the bed of wedlock, that thou wouldst come from Hell to seek me, but that I would come to thee from earth.

Then before she climbs upon the pile, she calls to those present to pile up the logs.

Pile up, good gentlemen, the oaken pile; let it stand high under the heaven. May my sorrow-laden breast burn, may the flame . . . . my heart . . . . may my sorrows melt away.

The Gleeman's Epilogue :—
>   May all gentlemen's griefs be bettered!
>   May all ladies have less of sorrow!
>   Now is Gudrun's CHAIN OF WOES told out.

HAMDISMÁL (WORDS OF HAMDIR)

Like Gudrun's Chain of Woes, this poem reflects Jordanes' story, but with considerably more detail. It is one of the oldest of the Eddic poems and the obscurities and probable lacunae may be explained in part by this circumstance.

I HEARD the bitterest bickering, hard words spoken forth of deep sorrow, when the stern-hearted Gudrun egged on her sons with fierce words.

'Why sit ye, why sleep ye your lives away? How can ye bear to speak words of cheer? Ye had a sister named Swanhild, whom Eormunrek trod down on the highway under the hoofs of his steeds, white and black, the grey well-broken horses of the Goths. Ye are not such as Gunnar, nor have ye hearts like Hogni's. Ye would have the will to avenge her if ye had the spirit of my brothers or the stern heart of the Hun-kings, yet ye are the sad remains of these great kings, ye only are alive, last strands of my race. I am left alone like an aspen in the wood; reft of my kinsmen like the fir of its branches; stripped of joy like a willow of her leaves when the branch-scather [the lopper with his bill] comes on a warm day.'

Then spake Hamtheow, the great of heart: 'Thou wouldst not have praised Hogni's deeds so highly when he and his fellows waked Sigfred from his sleep; thou wast sleeping in the bed, while the slayers laughed. Thy blue and white coverlets were dyed red with the gore of thy husband, bathed in his blood. When Sigfred sunk in death thou didst sit over him dead; thou hadst no mind for joy. Gunnar wrought that for thee. Thou thoughtest to pain Atli by the murder of Erp and by the slaying of Eitil; but thou hurtedst thyself. . . . One should so use the biting sword to slay another as not to hurt himself. The revenge of thy gladsome brothers was sharp and sore to thee when thou didst murder thine own sons therefore. . . . All united we might revenge our sister upon Eormunrek.'

Then spake Sorli, he had a wise mind: 'I will not bandy words with my mother; each of you still thinks a word is lacking. What dost thou ask for, Gudrun, which thou canst not speak for tears? Bring out the war-crests of the Hun-kings, now that thou hast egged us on to the court of swords!'

Gudrun turned to her storehouse, laughing; chose out of the chests the kings' crested helms and the long mail-coats and brought them to her sons. They shook their cloaks, they fastened their swords, and the god-born heroes clad themselves in goodly woven raiment, . . . and angrily sprung on their horses.

107

Then quoth Sorli, etc.... (*as they took leave of their mother*): 'Weep for thy daughter, and for thy sweet sons too, thy young children whom thou hast led into thy feud. Thou shalt have to bewail both of us, Gudrun, that sit here doomed on our horses; we shall die far away.'

Then quoth Hamtheow, etc.: 'We shall never come back to our mother [when we have slain the King of Goths]. Thou shalt drink the arval for us all together, for Swanhild and thy sons.'

They went out of the court foaming with rage; the young men rode on their Hun horses over the wet mountains to revenge the murder [of their sister]. They met on the street their [base brother]. 'How shall this little ... help us?'

He answered their half-brother, saying that he would help his kinsmen as foot does hand, or flesh-fast hand does foot....

They say: 'How may foot help hand, or flesh-fast hand help foot?'...

Erp the merry, as he sat on his horse's back, spake once: 'It is ill work to show cowards the way.'...

They said that the bastard was over-bold, they drew the [scathing] iron from the sheath ... with the edge of the sword they minished their strength by a third when they felled their young brother to the ground.

II.

The road lay before them, they found ... a wolf-tree [gallows] wind-cold on the west of the hall, and their sister's son wounded on the tree. The 'corse' kept swinging, ... it was not pleasant to stay there. They saw the Goths' hall and the lofty watch-seats, and Bikki's warriors standing within the high stronghold, the hall of the Southerners set round with seat-benches, with clasped targets and white shields. There was a clatter inside, the men were merry with ale, and the Goths paid no heed to their coming till the proud warrior blew his horn. The watchmen told Eormunrek that helmed men were in sight. 'Take counsel thereto, for they that come be mighty; it was the sister of the strong that ye have trodden [under your horse-hoofs].'

Then Eormunrek laughed, and stroked his beard, leant over to his leman, maddened with wine. He shook his brown hair; he looked on his white shield; he rolled the gold cup round in his hand. 'Happy should I think myself if I could see Hamtheow and Sorli in my hall! I would bind them with bow-strings, and fasten the god-born [heroes] to the gallows.' ... [*What has fallen out recounts the coming of the two brothers and their furious onslaught, no iron will bite on their mail, and they slay on the right hand and on the left. Eormunrek, weltering in his blood, his hands and feet cut off, shouts out in his rage*]: 'Shall not ten hundred Goths bind and beat down two lone men in the high hall!'

There was an uproar in the hall; the ale-cups were shivered; men lay in the blood that had flowed from the breasts of the Goths. Then spake Hamtheow, the stout of heart: 'Thou didst wish, Eormunrek, for the coming of us two brethren to thy stronghold. Now, Eormunrek, look at thy feet, look at thine hands cast into the burning fire.'

Then the god-sprung king roared mightily, as a bear roars, out of his harness: 'Stone ye these fellows, these sons of Ionakr, that spears will not bite nor sword-edge nor arrows!'

Then spake Hamtheow, stout of heart: 'It was ill done of thee, brother, to unloose the bag. Sharp counsels often come out of a shrivelled belly.'

Quoth Sorli: 'Thou hast heart enough, Hamtheow, would thou hadst wit to boot. It is a sad lack in a man to lack of wisdom.'

Quoth Hamtheow: 'The head would be off by now, if Erp had lived, our bold brother whom we slew on the way . . . the fairies egged us on, . . . set us to murder him.'

Quoth Sorli: 'I never thought that we two should come to do as the wolves do, and fly at one another, like the Fates' greedy greyhounds that are bred in the wilderness. . . .

INDEX

This index has been prepared primarily for the use of beginning students who may find variant forms of names (even within the translation of Vigfusson and Powell) confusing. There is an abundance of cross-references, often from names that do not appear in the text but which may be familiar from other sources (e.g., Götterdämmerung). When a cross-reference from a variant form falls next to the entry to which it refers, it is usually indicated in parenthesis following the main entry. The forms in Vigfusson and Powell are generally, but not invariably, the main entries. Thus there are apparent inconsistencies in the forms chosen for indexing, but the cross-references will help eliminate confusion on the part of the reader.

Cross-references from hl—, hn—, and hr— to l—, n—, and r—; from wr— to r—; from i to j; and from v to w, or vice versa, have been made whenever there is a chance for the uninitiated to be confused. However, many such references have been omitted as unnecessary, particularly when the two forms would be in immediate sequence in this index (e.g., Hialmar and Hjalmar).

113

114

Gold-weig, 15
Gollni, 64
Golltoppr, see Goldcrest
Gothland, 87, 105
Gothorm, 73, 79, 84, 88
Goths, 107, 108
Gothworm, 59
Gotland (Denmark, not
    the island now a part
    of Sweden), 58
Götterdämmerung (German),
    see Ragnarǫk
Gram, 74, 76
Grani, 64, 71, 82, 85, 87, 88,
    93
Granmar, 62, 64, 65
Gravedigger, 23
Grave-Wolf, 23
Greedy (Geri), see Wolves
    of Odin
Greenland Lay of Alti
    (Atlamál in Groenlenzka),
    98
Greyback, 23
Grim (a name of Odin), 24
Grimhild, 73, 89, 92, 102;
    Giuki's wife, Gudrun's
    mother; not to be
    confused with Kriemhild,
    the name of Gudrun in
    the Nibelungenlied
Grimm, Jacob, 1
Grímnir, 22
Grímnismál (Words of Grímnir),
    22
Gripir, 71, 72, 73
Gripisspá (Prophecy of
    Gripir), 71
Groa, 28
Grottasǫngr (The Mill Song),
    58
Grotte, 58
Gudrun (Kriemhild in the
    Nibelungenlied), 46, 72,
    73, 74, 79, 81, 82, 83,
    84, 85, 86, 87, 88, 89,
    91, 93, 94, 96, 97, 98,
    100, 101, 102, 103,
    104, 105, 106, 107,
    108
Gudrúnarkvida (Lay of
    Gudrun), 81

Gudrúnarkvida in Forna (Old
    Lay of Gudrun), 88
Gudrúnarkvida in Thridja
    (Third Lay of Gudrun),
    91
Gudrun's Chain of Woes
    (Tregrof Gudrúnar),
    105, 107
Gullinkambi (Gold-Comb),
    see Fialar
Gunnar (Gunther in the
    Nibelungenlied), 72, 73,
    79, 82, 83, 84, 85, 88,
    89, 92, 93, 94, 95, 96,
    98, 99, 100, 102, 105,
    107
Gunther, see Gunnar
Gylfaginning (first part of the
    Prose Edda), 2
Gylfi, 2
Gyllir (a horse of the Anses),
    23
Gymir (see also Eager, with
    whom Gerd's father is
    sometimes confused),
    37, 49, 51

H
For words beginning with
hl, hn, and hr that are not
located here look under
l, n, and r.

Hagal, 68
Hagen, see Hogni
Haid, 16
Hakon, 88
Halfdan, 60, 69
Hamal, 68
Hamdir, see Hamtheow
Hamdismál (Words of
    Hamdir), 107
Hamtheow (Hamdir,
    Ammius in Jordanes),
    105, 107, 108, 109
Hár, see High One
Hárbard (Hoarbeard, a name
    of Odin), 24, 34, 36
Hárbardsljod (Lay of
    Hárbard), 34, 40
Harding, 68, 69, 90

115

Modi, see Mood
Mogthrasi, Maids of (the
  Norns), 21
Moin, 23
Moin-land, 92
Moin's heath, 64
Mood (Modi), 21
Moon, 15, 16, 20, 26
Moon-Hound, see Garmr
Morris, William, 70
Mountain giants, see
  Giants
Muchwise, 29
Munarvoe, 55, 56
Munch, P.A., 2
Mundilfori (Fire-Auger),
  20
Munin (Mind), see Ravens of
  Odin
Murkwood, see Mirkwood
Muspell, 17, 51
Mysing, 58

N

Naglfar, see Nail-board
Nail-board (Naglfar), 17
Nari, 49
Nástrand, see Corse-strand
Necklace Glad, see Menglöd
Neri (a Norn ?), 62
Nerthus, see Niord
Niars, 46, 47, 48
Nibelungenlied, 53, 70, 94
Nibelungs, see Niflungs
Nidad, 46, 47, 48
Nidhogg, 18
Niflungs (Hniflungs,
  Nibelungs, Nibelungen),
  64, 70, 80, 94, 95, 100,
  101, 103, 105; essentially
  synonymous with
  Giukings (q.v.); see also
  Hoard of the Nibelungs
Night, 15, 20, 26
Nikar, see Hnikar
Niord (Nerthus in Tacitus,
  also spelled Njord),
  21, 24, 39, 44, 51
Noatun (Noaton, Noatown),
  21, 23, 44

Noble Deer (a name of
  Sigurd), 75
Norns (Fates; Urd, Verdandi,
  and Skuld), 21, 75, 76,
  98; also called Maids of
  Mogthrasi (q.v.); see
  also Neri, possibly a
  Norn
Norse Mythology, by
  Munch, 2
Norway, 56, 67
Norwi, 20, 26

O

Oakthorn (Eikthrynir), 23
Od, Maid of, 15
Oddrun (Ordrun), 85, 92
Oddrúnargrátr (Dirge of
  Oddrun), 92
Odin, 1, 3, 10, 16, 17, 19,
  22, 23, 24, 35, 38,
  40, 49, 50, 52, 53, 54,
  58, 62, 64, 65, 66, 74,
  82, 87
Odin's Love Lessons, 10
Odreari (inspiration), 11
Oin, 75
Okoln, 17
Old Lay of Gudrun
  (Gudrúnarkvida in
  Forna), 88
Opener (a name of Odin),
  24
Ordeal, trial by, 91
Ordrun, see Oddrun
Origins of Icelandic
  Literature, by
  Turville-Petre, 2
Orkning, 99
Orpheus, 53
Orwhelm (Aurgelmir), 20
Ostrogoths, 105
Otter, 74

P

Pale-Neb (the vulture), 17
Palna-toki, 46
Peace of Frodi, 58
Philoctetes, 46

119

122